A FEEL FOR THE GAME

D1491248

ALSO BY MELANIE HAUSER

Under the Lone Star Flagstick (ed.)

ALSO BY BEN CRENSHAW

Classic Instruction by Bobby Jones and Ben Crenshaw

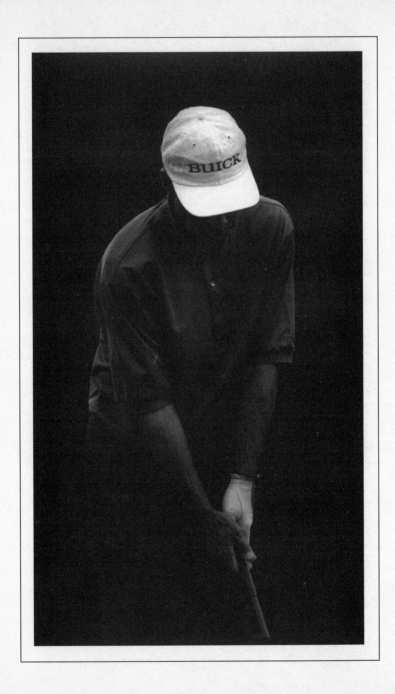

A FEEL FOR THE GAME

A MASTER'S MEMOIR

BEN CRENSHAW

with Melanie Hauser

BROADWAY BOOKS

new york

B BROADWAY

A hardcover edition of this book was originally published in 2001 by Doubleday, a division of Random House, Inc. It is here reprinted by arrangement with Doubleday.

A FEEL FOR THE GAME. Copyright © 2001 by Ben Crenshaw. All rights reserved. No part of this book may be reproduced or transmitted in any form or by any means, electronic or mechanical, including photocopying, recording, or by any information storage and retrieval system, without written permission from the publisher. For information, address Broadway Books, a division of Random House, Inc., 1540 Broadway, New York, NY 10036.

Broadway Books titles may be purchased for business or promotional use or for special sales. For information, please write to: Special Markets Department, Random House, Inc., 1540 Broadway, New York, NY 10036.

PRINTED IN THE UNITED STATES OF AMERICA

BROADWAY BOOKS and its logo, a letter B bisected on the diagonal, are trademarks of Broadway Books, a division of Random House, Inc.

Visit our website at www.broadwaybooks.com

First Broadway Books trade paperback edition published 2002

The Library of Congress has cataloged the hardcover edition as follows:
Crenshaw, Ben.
A feel for the game: to Brookline and back /
Ben Crenshaw.—1st ed.
p.   cm.
1. Crenshaw, Ben.   2. Golfers—United States—Biography.
I. Title
GV964.C74 A3 2001
796.352'092—dc21
00-065617

BOOK DESIGN BY AMANDA DEWEY

ISBN 0-7679-0622-5

1 3 5 7 9 10 8 6 4 2

To Dad and Harvey, who gave me a passion for golf;
and for all those who love the game.

CONTENTS

CONTENTS

INTRODUCTION
AND ACKNOWLEDGMENTS

The task of writing an autobiography, or more accurately a few of my experiences in life and golf, has been an interesting endeavor. I'm not really one to sit down with a tape recorder and talk for hours on end. I simply have too many things going on in my life to seclude myself and concentrate on just one project.

Recently I've been working with my architecture partner Bill Coore, on the Austin Golf Club right here in Texas, which will be my golfing home in the future. At the same time I've been trying to regain my enthusiasm for playing after spending two years preparing for the Ryder Cup matches in Boston. I have three precious daughters and a wonderful wife at home, where I try to spend as much time as possible.

And yet, after more than forty years of playing golf, I decided this was the time to write a book. I have surprised myself with the things that I remembered. Trying to capture my past has opened a floodgate of special memories and experiences.

I have been blessed with many friends, achievements, and honors in my life, and I owe them all to golf. Golf brought me closer to my father and introduced me to Harvey Penick, who taught me not only how to play the game but also so much about life. I've suffered heartache in the game, and not winning a major for my first eleven years on the Tour was difficult to accept given the number of good chances I had. But in the end the tough losses made my victories at Augusta even sweeter. My two Masters championships and numerous other tournament wins give me a great sense of pride. Winning the Irish Open, the World Cup, and playing on four Ryder Cup teams are also things I will never forget. Finally, having the chance to captain the United States team in Brookline, following a great legacy of captains, all of whom I've looked up to, was the pinnacle of my career. How could a golfer ask for more?

The lifelong friends I have made in golf will be with me well beyond my playing days. All of the acquaintances I have made over the years have confirmed to me that golf is indeed a gentleman's game and that the integrity of the ladies and men who play golf is unmatched in any sport.

No matter how hard I have tried to put my golfing life into perspective and on paper, the task would not have been possible without the help of many people. I have been fortunate during my career to know many talented journalists and writers—Herbert Warren Wind, Dave Anderson, Dan Jenkins, Charles Price, Jim Murray, and Bob Green to name just a few. When I set about selecting a writer to help me translate my thoughts into text, I had many excellent choices before me. Early on, I leaned on Thomas Bonk, golf writer for the *Los Angeles Times*, to help get me started. Later, because of timing issues, most of which were related to my schedule, I asked my good friend Melanie Hauser, who has written so much about me during my career, if she would step in to complete the project. Because Melanie lives in Houston and teaches a course at the University of Texas in Austin, we were able to spend a concentrated amount of time on the book during the late summer and fall of 2000.

My wife Julie has been a great help to me in recreating the months leading up to the Ryder Cup matches and that historic week in Boston as well as my second Masters win in 1995. She was right by my side during these wonderful times, and I must say her recollections were most helpful in recalling these events. My longtime friend and agent, Scotty Sayers, whom I have known for thirty-eight years, helped with topic and list suggestions, proofreading, and confirming details that long ago slipped my mind.

Along with Julie and Scotty, I had a great time putting together the photo section of this book, and just as with writers, over the course of my career I have been lucky to know many creative photojournalists. Jules Alexander, Fred Vuich, Robert Walker, Brian Morgan, Frank Christian, and Phil Sheldon have captured many highlights of my career. And my sister Bonnie gave me wonderful scrapbooks of my childhood that have always been dear to me and proved very useful in this book. And of course my brother Charlie, who helped jog my memory from time to time.

Many people too numerous to mention have been helpful with this project, but I must single out a few. The "girls" at the office, including Kimberly Johnson, Janet Miller, Deena Geltmeier, and Sonya Hursh, have been invaluable, as have Mickey Holden, Martin Davis, and Danny Pounds and his staff at Pounds Photography. Also, the photo departments at *Sports Illustrated*, *Golf Magazine*, *Allsport*, the *Boston Herald*, and *Golf Digest* have been most accommodating.

The whole process of putting my thoughts into the final product has been fascinating. My friends Ike Williams and Larry Moulter helped us through the interview procedure for a publisher, and I appreciate the relationship that I have established with the staff at Doubleday. My editor, Shawn Coyne, is one of the most patient people I have ever known. The lists at the beginning of each chapter were Shawn's idea. While my intent was to have a little fun sharing these with the reader, such lists have omissions by nature. The listings under each topic were arranged in no particular order.

While this book is my memoirs, the result is truly a team effort, and I sincerely thank everyone for their generous help and support.

A FEEL FOR THE GAME

PROLOGUE

(Ryder Cup tease, Brookline connection)

As I knelt beside the seventeenth green, my heart was pounding so hard it was about to fly right out of my chest. I closed my eyes and took a deep breath, but there was no way to settle myself down. A voice crackled in my ear. Was someone in trouble on another hole? I didn't know. I wasn't listening to whoever was on the other end of my walkie-talkie.

The only sounds I could hear were the deafening cheers from the fifteenth hole reverberating through the trees as Jim Furyk closed out his match.

The impossible was unfolding in front of me. To my right the scoreboard was a blaze of American red with just the barest hint of European blue. Two black flashes on the lower half of the board indicated that a pair of matches were all square—Stewart vs. Montgomerie, and the one playing out in front of me, Leonard vs. Olazabal.

If only, I thought. If only—Stewart or Leonard—could halve his match, it would be over. A half point was all we needed.

One halve and we would win the Ryder Cup.

I rested my arm on one knee and waited as Justin Leonard lined up his putt. Everything was in slow motion. I opened my mouth, but nothing would come out. I tried to focus on the line, on the moment, on the look on Justin's face, but my mind refused to settle down. I was too scared to think.

My gosh. If Justin can just halve this match, we're going to win the Ryder Cup.

The sunlight slashed through the trees and I tried to catch my breath. I'd rushed to get here from the eighteenth green, where Mark O'Meara had just lost a close match 1-up. It was all coming down to this. To an unbelievable finish. An exclamation point for one team on an absolutely fabulous day.

Moments came flooding back, unfurling so perfectly, so effortlessly, it seemed as though I was in the midst of a dream. There was Tom Lehman stepping to the first tee and hitting the purest drive—straight down the middle—I'd ever seen. Hal Sutton who had played such fabulous golf all week. David Duval's thirty-foot miracle on the tenth. Furyk's steady win. Payne Stewart throwing his hands up and celebrating with the crowd. Raymond Floyd shaking his head and murmuring that he could feel something happening in those old trees.

I thought about The Country Club. This seventeenth green and everything that had come to pass right here. About Francis Ouimet and his house that was a pitching wedge away from where I was kneeling, just over there on Clyde Street. About the 1913 U.S. Open, when Ouimet, a nineteen-year-old caddie and part-time sporting goods salesman, beat the best players in the game—Harry Vardon and Ted Ray of England—in a playoff that awakened the game in America. About

Ouimet's ten-year-old caddie, Eddie Lowery, whose only piece of advice all week was just to keep his eye on the ball. About the twenty-foot downhill putt for birdie that forced the playoff. About the birdie at that same seventeenth the following day that gave Ouimet the title and changed the face of the game.

It was so ironic, so fitting, that it would come down to this moment on this green. The place where a rich man's game had in one magic moment become a game for everyone; a stage today for what could be the greatest comeback in the history of the Ryder Cup.

My gosh. If Justin can just halve this match, we're going to win the Ryder Cup.

What kind of a strange and wonderful trip had I taken to arrive at this precise moment in time with so much at stake? After a lifetime in golf, after two years as Ryder Cup captain, after months filled with details and preparation, after surviving a nasty issue about money distribution that might have torn us completely apart, after falling a heretofore insurmountable four points behind the European team the first two days, it had come to this. To one putt by one player on *the* one hole that meant more to American golf than any other in history . . . and maybe to me, too.

Brookline wasn't just some small town on the outer edge of Boston. And The Country Club was no ordinary course. It was not only the scene of Ouimet's Open, it was where my dad had brought me to play my first U.S. Junior Amateur in 1968; where I had first been struck by the beauty and detail of a golf course; where I began to love the history of the game; where I realized there was so much more to golf than playing eighteen holes.

The Country Club had gone wild that day in 1913. No American golf gallery had ever witnessed such an event or watched such an unbelievable story unfold in front of them. A kid with a ten-year-old caddie beats the top two players in the game to win the U.S. Open on a course next door to his house—well, how can you possibly explain it?

Things just happen in this game. Things that make no sense; things you can't explain. Things that separate players in major championships; things that, when you feel everything is about to spin out of control, just seem to suddenly fall into place.

It may be as simple as a slight turn of the ball or the way it catches the barest edge of the cup and falls right into the hole. It can be a tree whose limbs part just enough to let a shot fly through; a piece of ground that kicks a ball back into a fairway when the only possible route is into the rough. They're shots that change the course of a tournament, a match, a player's life. Like that pitch-and-run Larry Mize hit in the dark at the 1987 Masters. Or Freddie Couples' tee shot at the twelfth at Augusta in 1992, when the ball stuck to the bank instead of rolling back into Rae's Creek. Or Bob Tway's bunker shot at the PGA Championship in 1986. You get the idea.

That's what makes golf so fascinating. Things happen unexpectedly. You ride out a storm that seems as if it could easily tear you apart, then suddenly you hole a bunker shot or a chip shot. You make two from the fairway. A sure two-putt falls in for birdie. A tournament, a match that seemed to belong to someone else, suddenly belongs to you.

Which brings us to right now. . . .

Down on one knee, everything in slow motion, with Justin lining up his putt. The entire team is there, or it seems that way. We all know what's at stake.

This was it. Europe had won the last two Ryder Cup matches—at Oak Hill in 1995 and at Valderrama in 1997. We had played well in those two matches—I was on the 1995 team—but the Europeans had played better. They had played together and always came up with big shots at just the right time. We just didn't.

There's certainly no disgrace in getting beat, but losing two in a row? The Ryder Cup is no longer just a friendly match that happens once every two years. It's one of the biggest sports events in the world and the pressure to win is intense. You're playing not just for yourself, but for your country. Your flag. Your teammates.

We were just plain tired of losing; of coming home shaking our heads and kicking ourselves; of wondering when we were going to capture some of that magic. We wanted to win, but there was no way the Europeans were going to roll over and just let us have the Ryder Cup.

I saw how losing had affected two close friends of mine—Lanny Wadkins and Tom Kite. They had captained the 1995 and 1997 teams, respectively, and they took their share of hits from the media. They were second-guessed for everything after they lost—Lanny especially for making Curtis Strange one of his captain's picks. Curtis had won the second of his back-to-back U.S. Opens at Oak Hill, the site of the '95 Ryder Cup, and was a good choice. But he just didn't play the way he wanted to. None of us did. We all shouldered the blame. And Tom? He was criticized unfairly, mostly, I might add, for letting Michael Jordan ride along in his golf cart. As if who was in the cart had anything to do with the outcome of the matches.

Then there was Seve Ballesteros. One of Europe's most dynamic and brilliant players and a Ryder Cup magician, some players on his team at Valderrama felt he was too demonstrative. But he won. So how can you criticize him for the results? Don't ask me why, but they did. What really counted wasn't the way he went about it, but that the Europeans played excellent golf as a team.

That Sunday, so did we. People forget that we came back from five points down that final day in 1997 and pushed the matches to the final hole of play. Believe me, that fact was not lost upon our team at The Country Club.

Losing? I never once thought about it. Neither did my assistants, Bruce Lietzke and Bill Rogers. It didn't enter into our conversations. We were concentrating on one thing:

My gosh. If Justin can just halve this match, we're going to win the Ryder Cup.

The putt was forty-five feet uphill with a couple of feet of break. I told myself we'd do well to halve this hole because Jose Maria's putt—from twenty-five feet—was eminently more hole-able. As Justin stood over the putt, I remember thinking that the best we could do here was halve the hole with a two-putt.

An eerie silence fell over the green as thousands of fans held their breath. Everyone was trembling—players, wives, caddies, me, the assistants.

We had started the day trailing Europe, 10–6, with only the twelve singles matches to go. All European captain Mark James had to do was somehow manage four points out of those twelve matches to reach fourteen points to clinch a tie and retain the cup. But we were in the midst of the greatest last-day comeback in history. With two matches left on the course, we led 14–12.

A half-point from Justin was all we needed.

When I think about it now, I can't help but smile . . . not necessarily because of the outcome, but because of the way fate always seems to step in.

I had that feeling all week. It wasn't an act. I believed that our team, our players, were destined for something more than a last-day rally that would fall short.

I knew that people were wondering if I had lost it Saturday night when I pointed my finger at the media and told them I had a good feeling about all of this. Down by four points and talking fate? They thought I was crazy. But somehow I knew.

All I had to do was follow the thread that runs through Brookline—Francis Ouimet, two American victories in the Walker Cup matches, Curtis winning his first Open in '88, my own experience in the Junior Amateur, and now the Ryder Cup. It was the perfect circle. It was a huge part of my life and golf history coming together.

Justin drew back his putter and the ball started to roll up toward the hole. As it crested the slope, I caught myself wondering if it was rolling too fast. I took a deep breath as it drew a bead on the hole. And the last four feet? I've never seen a ball with such eyes. The hole just swallowed it up.

The putt was an exclamation point to the most unbelievable

comeback in Ryder Cup history. It sent chills down everyone's spine and threw the world into orbit. I'm certain that people in downtown Boston could hear the cheers reverberate.

It was a moment that was absolutely in a dimension by itself.

It was fate.

1.

AUSTIN ROOTS

> BEST AUSTIN TRADITIONS
>
> *Cisco's Bakery for breakfast*
> *The Hoffbrau*
> *Dirty Martin's*
> *Lion's Municipal Golf Course*
> *Barton Springs*
> *UT Football*
> *Bert's Barbeque*
> *Jake's (sadly, no more)*
> *Butler Park Pitch & Putt*

When you're a kid, what do you need? A swimming pool. A backstop for baseball. A field big enough to get a football game going. A dirt road to ride bikes down. A front yard with trees laid out perfectly to serve as bases for the baseball game always underway. A mulberry tree whose branches provided the perfect escape for two brothers on a lazy Texas afternoon.

My brother Charlie and I used to climb that tree in our backyard at the end of the day and eat mulberries 'til our fingers turned purple. There was something wonderful about the taste, which changed with the seasons, and we always enjoyed the underlying certainty that one of us would get so carried away we'd pop one into our mouth before inspecting it for worms. It made for a lot of laughs and stomachaches during those years.

When you're six or seven there's no end to the fun you can have on a tree-lined *Leave It To Beaver* street like the one we grew up on in the Tarrytown area of West Austin. Rows of well-kept homes, trimmed hedges, and immaculate yards lined Bridle Path, where we lived in a cozy two-story home. The sprawling oaks in everyone's yard provided shade on a hot afternoon, and we even had a vacant lot nearby, the perfect place to build two forts about fifty yards apart and have all-world dirt-clod wars with your best friends. I can still feel the sting of those clods. Texas dirt has so much clay in it that dirtballs make unbelievable missiles.

There was nothing we didn't have back then, when kids didn't have a care in the world. All around us, everywhere we looked, there was something to do, something to keep us interested and challenged and, in my parents' view I suppose, occupied. Our neighborhood was filled with warmth, love, and fun. And, at our house, some kind of brotherly competition.

Charlie was just fifteen months older than me, so we grew up competing in everything. We shared a bedroom and a never-ending supply of teammates and friends, but he always seemed to be a head taller and a stride faster than me. So everything I got I had to earn. Like that old catcher's mitt.

I must have been six when I decided that my future was behind the plate. My dad had been a star catcher at Baylor, and Charlie was already one of the best Little League pitchers for his age in West Austin. So when I saw the perfect catcher's mitt in a catalog, I was convinced that the "hole" or pocket in the glove would catch the ball by itself. I was just eaten up with the thought of that mitt and kept pestering my dad for it, crawling up in his lap every night to show him a picture of it. He would always nod, but never say yes.

This went on for maybe two whole years until, one day, dad said if I could learn to catch Charlie, he'd get me that mitt. I begged Charlie unmercifully for three weeks—every day after school—until he gave in. Then, well, we wore out the lawn.

We found a perfect area, marked off the distance between the mound and home plate, and laid down towels that pretty well killed all the grass underneath and left us with the start of our front-yard diamond. Then Charlie started firing at me.

He threw balls at me into the dirt, over my head—anything but a strike. He had to make it tough on me and that little bitty glove I had that couldn't catch a thing—that's just what a big brother does to irritate you and leave a few bruises while he's at it.

After a few months I started catching him, so I called dad over one night when he came home. Charlie made it tough, but I caught every pitch he threw. And Dad? He went down to Rooster Andrews Sporting Goods and bought my mitt. Over the years we tore up the lawn in the front yard with all of our games. No hedge or flower was ever safe from us; there wasn't a sport that couldn't be played under those trees. We'd customize the field, using trees for bases, which turned dangerous the day Andy Loudermilk, one of our neighbors, was rounding third and knocked himself flat at the third-base tree.

We had only one television channel in those days—KTBC—so we made our own fun. If we weren't in the yard or on the street, we'd head over to West Enfield Park two blocks away to swim or play a pickup game with older guys like Chicago Cubs manager and longtime major leaguer Don Baylor, who started at center field for Austin High at the same time Charlie was a starter in right. Don used to hit rockets when we were kids, and we'd just stand there and ask him to hit it far. He would and we'd stand there duly amazed.

We moved into that house when I was four and it still looks the same. Oh, the trees are bigger and those bald spots in the lawn are all filled in, but the neighborhood—I live only a few blocks away—is still a kid's paradise. And the dads? Like mine, they coach.

My father Charlie was the perfect blend of discipline and tenderness. One day he'd be wearing me out about something I hadn't done; the next he was throwing that big old arm of his around my shoulder. Born and raised in Alabama, he looked so much like his old college suitemate and Sigma Nu fraternity brother Bear Bryant that people had trouble telling them apart. Especially since Dad used to play up the resemblance by wearing one of Bear's signature houndstooth hats. And, when people asked what kind of a team he'd have next year at 'Bama, he never passed up a chance to tell them everything they wanted to know.

Dad spent only one year at 'Bama before transferring to Baylor, where his younger brother Allen was in pre-med. I don't know what possessed him to stay in Texas after graduation, but I do know what kept him here—my mother, Pearl Vail Johnson. He was practicing law in Houston when he met my mother, who had graduated from the University of Houston and was teaching elementary school. They were living in the same boardinghouse in the Montrose area and everyone in the house kept trying to fix them up. They resisted for a while, but once they got together, it wasn't long before they fell in love and were married—at that same boardinghouse. Mom, a fine piano player, played at her own wedding.

Not long after they married, my dad was offered a job at the attorney general's office in Austin, and the Crenshaw roots in the capital city were permanently established. He served Governor Price Daniel, whose brother Bill had roomed with Dad in law school, and they became so close that when I was born, they named me Ben Daniel Crenshaw. Yes, after the governor.

My mother taught school in Austin while Dad represented a lot of companies, including 3M, in front of the state legislature, but his passions were golf and baseball. He loved baseball and coached Charlie and me when we were growing up. And it didn't stop there. When Charlie played baseball at Texas, Dad was always in the stands, usually picking up a few tips while sitting with legendary UT baseball coach Bibb Falk.

Dad had a great way of making a point. When I was about eight

I wanted a new rod and reel, so Dad used that to improve my batting stance. I had a habit of "stepping in the bucket," especially against older pitchers I feared, and Dad was going to break me of it. He said, "Until you step towards that pitcher with your left foot, you're not getting that rod and reel." One day I stepped forward and got a really good base hit—and that rod and reel. That was his way. He would make us work hard and do something he wanted us to do so he could tell that we were learning. Then we would get a reward.

And, he was so kind to everyone. He made the whole team feel ten feet tall—no matter who was the star that day. He touched so many lives, and many guys I played sports with have gone on to coach Little League and soccer and kickball themselves—even me.

One thing that really touched me was, about three months before Dad died, he was carrying a little letter around in his pocket that Jerry Bell, a Houston attorney who had played on our Little League team, had written him. It was a beautiful, sweet little letter remembering the years in West Austin Little League and telling Dad that, as he coached his daughter and her softball team, all he could think about was wanting to coach like Dad. It made Dad very proud.

Dad loved everything about baseball and so did Charlie and I. So you can imagine how excited we were when Dad decided to take us to St. Louis on the train to see a Cardinals–Cubs game at old Busch Stadium. Dad had a friend from law school who knew Stan Musial and he arranged it so we could meet him. We got to meet Ernie Banks, too, and shake their hands and eat at Biggie's—Stan Musial's restaurant just outside the stadium. Imagine that as kids. We thought we were in heaven for those five days.

The whole trip back, Charlie and I—dressed up in our "good" clothes because that's the way you traveled back then—ran all over the train. We wore Dad out. I think he was glad to get us back home.

Honestly though, while growing up we were surrounded by an unbelievable cast of characters. We played baseball and football with the sons of governors, politicians, and coaching legends.

I remember in 1963, Mark Connally, the son of Texas governor John Connally, was in school with us. President Kennedy was supposed to fly to Austin later that day and we were going to get out of school early. Just after lunch two state troopers came to school and took Mark and Scotty Sayers, now my agent and business manager, out of school. Scotty's dad worked for the governor at the time and we didn't know what to make of it. When school got out we learned that President Kennedy had died in Dallas and that Mark's father had been wounded.

We lived and died with the University of Texas Longhorns because we knew football coach Darrell Royal and his staff. We were touched by many great events and people, which is just the way it is when you're raised in the state capital and in the shadow of one of the finest universities in the country. But often it was years before we knew the stories behind some of the faces.

One night Dad brought home this short, balding man and called us away from one of our front-yard games. "Boys," he said, "I want you to meet D. X. Bible." Charlie and I didn't know who he was, but he handed us a brand new J5V1 football with The University of Texas written on it. He told us he wanted us to take that ball and scuff the heck out of it. We did.

Bible had a sweet spot and came back a few other times, each time bringing us a new ball, but it wasn't until later that I found out he was one of the most legendary and prominent coaches UT ever had. To me and Charlie, he was the guy with the footballs.

And there was Wilmer Allison, a 1930s tennis star, two-time U.S. Open doubles champ with John Van Ryn, and former UT coach, who was another of Dad's friends. Colonel Allison had a group that always met at four in the afternoon for their putting match at old Austin Country Club. Without fail, Mr. Allison would show up with his old Ben Hogan putter in one hand and his glass of "lemonade" in the other. I used to laugh about how much he liked those lemonades, which I later learned were laced with vodka.

Dad played in those games and so did Walter Benson, a tremendous ball striker who couldn't putt worth a lick—poor soul. The fourth player was Ted Whitlock, who always putted with the same ball. It was so old it was yellow; so worn and slick you could hardly see where the dimples once were. I used to watch them putt for hours, going around and putting different putts, Mr. Allison sipping "lemonade" and the whole group laying down a few friendly bets along the way.

It was a game, and Harvey Penick, of course, loved for people to play games. Harvey . . . there's so much to say about him and his teachings, but for the moment, I'll just remind you that he was the pro at Austin Country Club. He took the job at age seventeen and was still teaching when he died in 1995.

Harvey thought people learned golf by playing games—whether it was eighteen holes, a chipping contest, or one of Mr. Allison's afternoon matches. There was no better way, and if he saw the same person putt the same putt ten times or work on the same shot for hours, he would wander over and tell him not to do that. "What you're doing for that particular putt is good," he would say, "but will you ever have this particular putt again in your life? Every putt you hit from now until the day you die is different. So why not hit different putts?

"Learn your touch, learn your speed, and learn to put pressure on yourself in a simple little competition."

That was beautifully simple to me. And it was exactly what Mr. Allison and his group were doing.

By that time Harvey had put my first club—a cut-down mashie—in my hands, and golf was beginning to wear spots of its own in the front yard. Golf was also not too kind to the windows in the area, some of which were taken out by a stray swing or two. That's when Mom made certain we stopped hitting real golf balls in the yard and switched us to Wiffle balls. For certain they could make their way into uncharted territory—and often did—but they didn't break anything in the process.

When we took up golf, Charlie of course was better than me. But we both loved it and would spend hours hitting—or at least trying to hit—shots.

Not long after Harvey gave me that first club and I started making time between baseball and football to practice, Mr. Allison decided that I needed my first putter, so he gave me a little hickory-shafted Burke putter. He claimed that Bobby Jones had given him the putter, but it didn't look at all like Calamity Jane because it didn't have a gooseneck.

Calamity Jane was a Winton given to Jones by a member of the Nassau Country Club. He later had Tom Stewart, a club maker at St. Andrews who made his irons, make copies of it. But the one I had wasn't even a copy.

I learned to putt with that old club and, just maybe, a little of Jones rubbed off on me all those years ago. I reshafted it to adult size, but I have been thinking about cutting it back down to the kid-size it once was because that putter and Jones have meant so much to my career. Ironic, isn't it, that a club I first touched fortysomething years ago still touches my heart.

My whole childhood was like that. From Dad, who would call up at the last second and inform us he was bringing four home for dinner, to my mother who had the patience of Job and a way—usually—of making everything better, to my sister Bonnie, who was ten years older than me, smart as a whip, had a wicked sense of humor and, I really think, just tolerated Charlie and me. We did everything little brothers are supposed to do—get into all her things, burp when her boyfriend came to the house, bother her to no end—and she loved us nonetheless. Bonnie is married now, a librarian in Montgomery County, just north of Houston, with two great boys, and sometimes I think she still just tolerates us.

My mother? She was the sweetest woman who ever lived—and along with Harvey was one of the two kindest souls I've ever known. I know that sounds like a son talking, but just ask around Austin.

Everyone who knew her would tell you the same thing. She taught sixth grade at Brykerwoods Elementary—Charlie and I went to Casis Elementary—and played piano at Sunday school and assorted parties where she and Jimmy Demaret would team for songs long into the night. She was so loving, so giving, so practical. There wasn't anything she wouldn't do for us.

She was a good athlete herself growing up in Virginia and I've thought I may well have inherited some of my touch and feel from her. Of course, we loved her cooking—what son can turn down a great southern meal like tuna casserole, fried chicken, or fresh vegetables every night?—and her smile. She always had a smile on her face. Plus, she had a great sense of humor and was always making up these little limericks and verses to entertain Charlie and me. She could make a limerick out of anything. Even ketchup—"Shake and shake the ketchup bottle, none will come and then a lot'll."

But even Mom had her breaking point. She would only take so much—especially from me and Charlie—and then she put her foot down. And the whole house knew it. She'd cut us so much slack and then we'd push her just a little too far. She'd come out front, grab a switch off the bush, and take off after us. And, believe me, she connected many times.

I laugh now, but it wasn't too funny back then. Neither were those rough days when nothing would go right and it seemed as though nothing could make you feel better. Nothing, maybe, but Mom.

My first three days at Austin High someone stole my lunch right out of my locker. It wasn't your basic lunch, mind you, but a Dagwood sandwich—you know, a sandwich two times the size of any sandwich you've ever seen, stuffed with just about everything in the refrigerator from lettuce to salami, tomatoes, cheese, mustard and . . . you name it.

Anyway, my locker was in a hallway underneath the street that connected the old part of the school to the new part, and someone summarily stole those Dagwoods. For three days.

I came home the third day with a sad look on my face and Mom said, "What happened, Bennie?" I told her and she said, "Oh, that's terrible."

Fifteen minutes later she came back. "I think I have a way to fix this," she said. "I'll make a Thor sandwich."

Thor was our dog—a Norwegian elkhound who spent most of his time in our backyard. That's where Mom got the fixins for the sandwich—three-day-old Thor reminders, the kind you slice, put between slices of bread with a little lettuce and cheese and no one would ever know. Until they bit into it.

I took it to school the next day and it was stolen. But it was the last time it was stolen.

We laughed hard about that for many years. That was Mom. She and Dad were so affectionate, so loving. We were so lucky. Hugs every morning and every night. And those special moments like making a Thor sandwich, or the afternoon no one would play golf with me or pay me any attention.

I was so upset that I walked over to Muny—the real name is Lion's Municipal Golf Course, but no one in Austin ever called it anything but Muny—and started playing by myself. I had just teed off on the fourth hole when I looked up and saw Mom coming over the hill.

"Bennie," she said softly, "I knew that you were alone and I wanted to be with you."

She died of a heart attack in 1974, but there's not a day that goes by that I don't think of her—and that moment. It's something I will cherish forever.

Dad's gone, too. We lost him two years ago after a long battle with thyroid cancer. He remarried after Mom died and for the next twenty years, he prided himself on his cooking. He'd go to the grocery store three times a day and to the farmers' market. He was always after the perfect tomato. He was going to get a jump on everybody and get the perfect black-eyed peas or onion or whatever. His favorite time—other than Masters week, of course—was the early summer when all the vegetables came out. It was a huge part of his life. As a matter of fact, half of his funeral service was spent talking about dad's food because his favorite thing was to gather this food and then visit his friends to give it away. He loved doing that.

And when there was a big pecan crop he would take pecans to everybody. He once even told my wife Julie that she was "un-American" because she didn't care for pecans. He was something else.

I miss them terribly, but I have them in my heart—and have a little of both of them in me.

2.

HARVEY

HARVEY'S THINGS TO
WORK ON

Proper Grip
Stance
Ball position
Club-face position
YOUR swing
Short game

As far back as I can remember, our conversations always ended the same way.

Harvey would extend his hand in a most unusual way, turning it so his palm was facing upward. I would take it lovingly, placing my hand over his and squeezing it for a few moments. Not too hard, not too soft. Just enough pressure to let him know how much he meant to me. How much he had meant for so many years.

Harvey never wavered. He would always pause for a moment, letting those decades of lessons sink in and leaving those two hearts to touch each other once again before he would lift his head a bit and say simply, "Take dead aim."

For nearly forty years we ended our visits with that little hand-shake. Except that last time. Harvey was in bed that Sunday afternoon as he had been for months and didn't hold his hand out. I guess he knew he didn't have to; that he'd done all he could.

"Go into the closet and get that old putter," he said not long after I arrived at his house. He checked my grip. My setup. And for the next few minutes he watched me swing that old hickory-shafted Gene Sarazen across the bedroom carpet.

"I want you to take two practice strokes and see to it that your hands don't pass the clubhead," he said from his bed. "All you need to do is trust."

Harvey always searched long and hard for his words; for how and what to say to people. He would study the pupil once he held out his hand to shake it. He would study your countenance. Before the lesson began he knew what kind of person you were. And what you needed.

He was so frail by that Sunday his skin was almost transparent; his eyes seemed lost more than ever in all those wrinkles. But he was as sharp as ever. He knew what he was doing; that he didn't have to say another word that day. He knew, somehow, it would be our last visit. But he knew, too, a part of him was going with me.

Seven days later, Harvey died.

Another seven days passed and I won my second Masters—this one with Harvey's hand resting on my shoulder.

Harvey was so special. There wasn't a kinder man in this world. He was the most kind, gentle man I ever met, and hopefully I inherited a little of his kindness. I wish I could have inherited more of his patience, but he gave me the love for the game and for people. He really made us all sort of look at people no matter who they were, who loved golf, in the same way. Whether it was a caddie or a governor, a club member or a maintenance man at Muny, Harvey had an uncanny way of putting people on the same level and treating them with equal parts of dignity and respect. That was evident to us even when we were youngsters.

Everyone knew Harvey went to church every Sunday. That was a huge part of his life. But it didn't stop there. He never spoke about religion, but he lived his faith. It came out of his life in every step he took. Kindness, compassion, respect, patience, dignity, pride, work, ethics, play by the rules. You name it. For all those reasons and so many more, everyone loved him.

Harvey never spoke a harsh word. He spoke so softly, I never remember him raising his voice. And he had an unbelievable way about him and a love for the game that he nurtured in everyone around him.

I met Harvey when I was six, and just by looking at him I could tell that he spent all his time outside, teaching at the golf course. The reason? Harvey was a very thin man but he had more wrinkles than anybody we ever knew because that sun baked his tough skin every day as he stood on the range.

"Harvey," Jimmy Demaret always said, "had so many wrinkles his face would hold a seven-day rain."

Those wrinkles just added to his character though. I remember that he seemed old even back then. He had taken the job at Austin Country Club when he was seventeen and coached the University of Texas golf team from 1931 to 1963. Can you imagine? The people at the country club had him for almost seventy years and they knew they were the lucky ones. Funny, but Harvey always thought he was the lucky one.

Harvey had been teaching my dad, so he would see Charlie and me tagging along. When he saw my obvious interest, he asked Dad if he could make a club for me and did, cutting down that little mashie— an old 5-iron—to size. He fashioned a small, slender grip out of leather and it fit my hand perfectly. When it was ready, Dad and Harvey took me to the practice tee and Harvey put my hands on the club.

"Now, keep them there," Harvey said, as Dad nodded in agreement. "Just keep your hands there."

That's just what I've done, for all these years.

Occasionally I would hit a shot with that little mashie when I was tagging along with Dad, but not too often. Usually Charlie and I would wait around for him, and Harvey finally told us to go down to the little chipping green tucked beside the first hole. It was a little green surrounded by pecan trees and one or two little bunkers and we spent hours down there—first with my mashie and Charlie's 3-iron; later on with our ragtag sets of clubs. To us it was paradise—somewhere to hit shots and learn and never get yelled at for holding up play.

The bottom line was that Harvey didn't want anyone on the golf course until he thought they were ready to play. It was part of the way he taught, but we just saw it as fun.

I can still see Harvey's tiny old shop tucked down past a little grotto area below the club and surrounded by trees and a rock wall. It was a dark, damp little room, maybe forty or fifty feet deep and twenty feet wide, that smelled of leather, grip solvent, and old wood-shafted clubs. The flooring was that old, green, spongy rubber that fit together like a puzzle so golfers could walk down there in cleats.

Harvey never had much inventory—a few shirts, a couple of boxes of shoes, and some clubs along the wall. A big pro shop wasn't for him. Give him a place to work on clubs and sell buckets of range balls and a desk for his lesson book. That was all Harvey needed.

Charlie and I wandered down there and saw all those balls. All we could think was, "Hey, a bunch of balls. Let's practice." So we took them and hit them. And came back and took more.

Just about that time, Dad came back in from his round. "What are y'all doing?" he asked. "Y'all are just taking those balls. I need to sign a ticket for them. They're not free."

Harvey was sitting at his desk and looked at Dad with a smile. "They're okay, Mr. Crenshaw," he said. "If they want to hit the balls, they're welcome to them. Let them hit them."

I know there are stories across the country about kind old gentlemen like that. Those are the people who live with you forever. Harvey was all about helping people and nurturing their love for the game because he knew it was a good game that served people well.

"Ol' Harvey," Dad always said, "is just as tender as a dove's heart."

Like so many professionals of his vintage, Harvey was always there—and always in so many different places. You looked up, and there was Harvey. If he wasn't on the putting green he was starting members on the first tee, or on the practice tee giving lessons. He was a fixture.

Back then and to a great extent now, a club professional has to wear many hats. Harvey was part of that age group just past the era of immigrants—of English and Scottish professionals who came to the country around the turn of the century. He believed in men like Stewart Maiden and Willie Campbell; in their way of teaching. They taught people how to play, worked on clubs, built clubs. They were part greenskeeper, part teacher, part businessman, and most were darned good players, too. They were encouragers; men who looked after the people and the youth of the game.

Those men believed there were certain fundamentals, a certain knowledge and skill level, required of players first. That's why Harvey wanted people hitting shots on the practice tee or chipping and putting around the green. He wanted to know a little bit more about a person. He wanted to help them learn and love the game, not just teach them how to hit a golf ball.

Harvey never really gave me a formal lesson, so to speak, when I was a junior. In fact, I'm not sure he ever gave me one. After he put my hands on that club, he would watch and only suggest something occasionally. He would look at our grips, sure, but I always knew what he wanted. He wanted to see that we could play a little chip shot. When I read his book I found out why. He said that if somebody can play a proper chip shot and contact the ball properly with their hands just a little bit ahead of the clubshaft—it's the same sensation as taking a full swing with your hands a little ahead of the ball at impact.

How simple is that? He wanted us to learn not to scoop or lift the ball into the air. He wanted us to know how to play different shots with that little club, and we obliged. I was always trying to hit every shot I could imagine. I could loft the ball pretty good with it, make it run when I wanted to, and hit it a certain distance and everywhere in between. Those are things no one can teach you. You learn by doing. And, by watching others.

Let me tell you, Harvey knew what he was doing. He wasn't an educated man. As far as I know he attended school only through the eighth or ninth grade, but he read a lot and learned words that would help him communicate with his pupils. Harvey and his brother Tom had caddied at the original Austin CC when they were growing up, and when Harvey was seventeen the members thought so much of his honesty and trustworthiness they offered him the head professional job.

Today Austin Country Club is nestled in the limestone hills of northwest Austin in a scenic setting overlooking Loop 360. But that's not the club where I grew up playing, or even the original ACC. The first site—where Harvey first caddied—was just off what's now I–35, where nine-hole Hancock Municipal Golf Course and Hancock Shopping Center, site of the original other nine holes, sit. The second Austin Country Club, where I grew up, was built just off Riverside Drive in southeast Austin in 1952. Back then, Harvey and his wife Helen lived in a little house that backed up to the par-three twelfth hole on what's now Penick Drive.

The club moved again, in 1984, to the current Pete Dye-designed course, and the course where I grew up became part of the Austin Community College complex. A group of us tried to influence the University of Texas to buy the course but it didn't work out, and that layout I loved has been radically altered and is now dotted with new parking lots and buildings.

The old course was a wonderful par 70 that you could get around without losing a ball. The huge old oak tree near the first tee is where we could usually find Harvey—standing beneath its branches, holding his trademark clipboard, and sending groups out onto the course. Not far away was that green where Charlie and I whiled away the hours.

From the very beginning I enjoyed putting. Harvey made it fun with those games he wanted us to play, and he was always encouraging us to putt each other a penny or a nickel or a Coca-Cola. No matter how many holes we played—and it was usually twenty-seven or thirty-six in the summer—we'd end the day playing these games on the putting green.

I loved putting because it was just plain fun, and it fascinated me to watch the ball roll over those blades of grass. Harvey never called it the most enjoyable shot in golf, not in so many words, but we all knew it was important because he was always encouraging us to do it. And, let's face it, sinking a putt is something all golfers enjoy.

Sometimes I wonder if Harvey knew me better than I did myself. Every time I ask myself that question, the answer is he probably did. He was there to put my hands on the club, there when I learned to hit shots and win tournaments. He was just trying to nurture everyone's golf—not only mine, but everybody's. He was doing all he could to get people interested in the game and then keep them playing.

As far as I know, Harvey never did care about money. It wasn't a part of his life. When he came out with his *Little Red Book* and the others in that series with Bud Shrake, his family started making just a little bit of money toward the end of his life. It was a first for him because he never really had made much money. In fact, he was still giving lessons for fifteen dollars in the 1990s—at least that's what he told Michael Jordan when Jordan called to book a lesson. The only thing that Harvey ever said about making all that money from his books was that he could now go into a restaurant and not have to choose from the right side of the menu.

If Harvey had three meals a day and a place to teach, he was content. He treated everyone the way he wanted to be treated and once told me, "As long as I am helping people, that is what makes me happy."

Can you imagine someone in this day and age with that kind of philosophy?

Harvey's teaching reflected his lifestyle—basic and simple. He believed that a correct grip, stance, and setup were the most important things he could teach a golfer, and he was a real stickler for a proper grip.

"If you don't have a good grip, you don't want to play good golf," he always said.

Simple, straightforward playing information. That was Harvey. Learn the little shots first because half the shots in the game are around the green. I don't care how good you are or how poorly you hit the ball, that message doesn't change. You can be a match for someone if you can putt halfway decently. If you miss a green, you can chip the ball right up there.

Harvey liked to quote Willie Park, saying, "A man who can putt is a match for anyone, and a man who cannot is a match for no one."

This man touched everyone he met in a way they could never forget with his manner, his simplicity, his gentleness. And in Dad's case, his patience.

Dad was a good player, but every player in the world—and I don't care who it is—at one time or another in his career gets a case of the shanks. And when Dad's case came, it was so bad he went to Harvey and asked him to take a look. Harvey took him to the practice tee and Dad proceeded to hit seventeen shanks in a row with a 7-iron. After seventeen shanks, Dad was beside himself. He looked at Harvey and Harvey looked at him.

"Mr. Crenshaw, I think we'd better tackle this tomorrow," Harvey said. That was it. Nothing more.

The next day they came out and Harvey suggested something to correct the problem. Can you imagine somebody watching seventeen shanks in a row and not saying anything? That's how patient Harvey was . . . silent after seventeen consecutive shanks.

So much of what I am now and who I am is because of Harvey. From members to dishwashers, everyone he touched at ACC benefited from his guidance.

I often wonder how different my life would have been if there had been no Harvey Penick to add to it. But it's not just me. He taught great pros on both the PGA Tour and the LPGA Tour—Tom Kite, Terry Dill, Don and Rik Massengale, Kathy Whitworth, Sandra Palmer, Betsy Cullen, Betsy Rawls, Judy Kimball, Peggy Wilson, and Cindy Figg-Currier. We're all better for having him in our lives.

By the way, I've still got that little cut-down 5-iron that he made for me all those years ago and I have that Sarazen putter. The putter was going to be buried with Harvey, but his son Tinsley gave it to me, which meant so much. Both clubs are in my study at home, not far from the trophy case that houses my two Masters trophies, which is only fitting. He saw me win one; his hand guided me through the other.

He helped more than he would ever know.

3.

TO BROOKLINE

FAVORITE U.S. OPEN VENUES

Shinnecock Hills
Pinehurst
Olympic
Oakmont
Pebble Beach
The Country Club

It was just a little gift, something from a father to his fifteen-year-old son. A chance to open my heart and mind to a game I had really taken to; an opportunity to glimpse into the past and, I think Dad hoped, peer into my future.

As I flipped through those pages of Charles Price's *The World of Golf*, I began to look beyond my afternoons at Austin Country Club and Muny. I started to dream of elegant clubhouses in beautiful settings and began to understand the rich history and colorful stars of the game of golf. Dad gave it to me as an incentive to make it to the U.S. Junior Amateur field the following summer. It would be played in Brookline at a place called The Country Club, one of the first clubs in

America and one which, at that point, stuck in my mind because of its primrose yellow clubhouse.

Until that moment my whole world had revolved around West Austin. Knebel Field, where we played Little League. Austin Country Club. Casis Elementary. O. Henry Junior High. And that slice of golf heaven at 2901 Enfield Road—Muny. Muny was less than six blocks from my house, next door to Knebel Field and right across the street from O. Henry. It was a shady, tight little course built as a WPA project during the Roosevelt administration by Harvey's brother Tom.

It was where Danay Covert once launched a homer out of Knebel Field that landed on the second green. It was where, if you sliced your tee shot on the twelfth, you yelled that it was headed for Dale Baker's barbecue joint, one of those places with sawdust on the floor and great sliced beef sandwiches. It was where I won my first tournament—the Casis Elementary fourth-grade tournament—with a blistering 46 for nine holes. It was where I won the 1969 Firecracker Open with the best ball-striking round of my life.

And, it was where I had my first hole in one, which is sort of like your first kiss. You never forget it.

I've hit better shots in my life, but that little 5-iron to the fifth hole was still one of the sweetest. Seeing that ball disappear was incredible. Especially since I was all of thirteen.

Strange, but two days later, I had another ace—this one on the eleventh at Muny.

Of course, you could always find us there during my junior high years. Can you imagine anything more convenient than a golf course right across the street from your school? Especially when you're in the seventh, eighth, and ninth grades? All I had to do was hop the fence, pay the quarter green fee, and tee it up. I was obsessed. When Bonnie would drive me to junior high, I'd tell her it wasn't fair that I had to waste a whole day in school when I could be out there playing golf.

When you didn't see me in school, it wasn't as if I were AWOL or anything. Everyone knew where I was—out there just knocking golf balls around, as usual. Charlie and I and anyone else who wanted to show up had sort of a regular routine. We would play all day and then come back to the clubhouse and practice on the putting greens until dark. We all loved to putt and, with Harvey over at Austin CC for inspiration, we were soon playing nine-hole contests for really high stakes—a carton of milk and a Bruce's pecan pie that we would get out of the vending machine for a quarter. We'd either play until somebody owned us or somebody showed up to take us home.

All Texas courses have colorful characters and tales associated with them, and Muny was no exception. One of the best involved legendary golf hustler Titanic Thompson, who, it seems, once bet some pigeon that he could throw half a pecan shell over the roof of the two-story clubhouse. The guy took Titanic up on the bet and, of course, Titanic flipped the shell over the roof with ease. It turned out that Titanic had filled that pecan shell with lead.

Even the not-so-famous had their place at Muny. Like Dudley Krueger, a janitor at the University of Texas, who wore khaki pants and a T-shirt and pulled a cart when he played. Dudley caught a lot of fellows by surprise because he didn't really look like much of a golfer, but could he play. He was a trick shot artist that Harvey always told us to watch. And when we'd ask him what he shot, he would mumble under his breath "something around 66."

It was an ideal situation for a kid—especially for a kid who loved to putt. I learned on the coarse Bermuda greens at Muny and the bentgrass greens at Austin Country Club, and the old theory is if you learn to putt on Bermuda, you can learn to roll the ball consistently on any surface. Bermuda has thick blades that affect the ball's line as it travels across them, and they force you to find which direction is west because Bermuda grows toward the setting sun. If you're putting against the grain, the coarse dark blades are going to hold the ball up. But if the grain is shiny, then you are going with the grain and will have a faster putt.

Bermuda grass putts require solid pace and line, while on bent grass you mostly just play the contour of the green. Why? Bent grass is just a finer, softer-bladed grass and doesn't have any grain to it. So having that combination to practice on helped me learn to read greens and putt, and having two such diverse courses, period, accelerated my development as a golfer.

Muny was tighter, had more trees, and forced you to keep the ball in play. Austin Country Club, one of the last courses Perry Maxwell designed, was a little wider so you could let it out. I loved Maxwell's greens and don't believe there was a finer green builder in the world. Early in his career Maxwell worked with Dr. Alister MacKenzie for four years and, although MacKenzie referred to Maxwell as his "Midwest associate" on his company stationery, Maxwell never got the credit he deserved. He worked with MacKenzie on Crystal Downs in Michigan, the University of Michigan, and Ohio State courses, and he rebuilt several greens at Pine Valley, Merion, and Augusta. After MacKenzie died in 1934, Maxwell designed Southern Hills, the site of the 2001 U.S. Open.

Those afternoons at Muny were teaching me how to compete and honing my skills as a putter. And looking back, I was a sponge—a towheaded, eager little sponge soaking up everything it could about the game. I was also beginning to play some pretty good golf.

One afternoon I shot 74 and came home about to bust, and Dad looked at me real funny.

"Are you sure you shot a 74?" he said. I told him I was certain I had.

"Well, son, I want you to sit down and go through the round shot by shot." So I did.

He just wanted to make sure I was being honest about my score and to make sure I was keeping up with all of my shots, and in fact, it turned out that I had. Another time, when I shot 68 at age thirteen, he sat me down again and we went through the round shot by shot. He could tell that his lessons about honesty took, as one day when I was sixteen I shot a 66 at Pecan Valley in San Antonio despite calling a two-stroke penalty on myself for accidentally kicking the ball. Dad was prouder that I called the penalty on myself than about the 66.

He was also a stickler for the rules. One day, I must have been nine or ten, we were playing with Dad at the club and I knocked it in the hole with a 9-iron from fifty yards out. A woman playing the sixth hole saw it and came over to give me fifty cents.

"Don't you accept that!" Dad bellowed, seeing rules violations dancing in his head. "You can't accept that. You're an amateur."

Years later it was Dad who came perilously close to crossing a line. Whenever I played the thirteenth or fifteenth hole at Augusta, he had a habit of kneeling down, cupping his hands, and yelling, "Lay up, lay up!" If that doesn't constitute advice from the gallery, I don't know what does. He was just beside himself every time I got near water—I did get wet more than my share of times—but eventually I had to ask him to suffer in silence so an official wouldn't slap me with a violation.

While Charlie and I were learning golf, Dad encouraged us to play other sports as well. In fact, I played on the basketball, football, and track teams at O. Henry and played baseball every spring. But for me, golf was becoming the most important thing in my life.

I've always been a person who, once I got interested in something, there was no stopping me. When I was really young it was birds. By the time I was seven I could tell you the markings and colors of most species in Texas. Bonnie used to drive me to the Texas Museum of History on the UT campus just so I could see the huge bald eagle there. I would get so excited it drove her crazy. And when Charlie took his BB gun and opened fire on some robins down the street one day? I chased after him screaming, "Murderer!" and tried to stop him. I couldn't. I carried one of the dead robins home—crying all the way—and laid it on the kitchen table. Mom felt so sorry for me she helped me lay it in a shoe box and bury it in the garden.

I was even more intense about golf. Especially the competition.

Once at a junior partnership tournament at Austin Country Club, I partnered with Joe Hornaday in a match against Charlie and his partner, Bobby Seaholm. The match went to extra holes, and Bobby, who had a fiery temper, was suddenly putting with a club that was no more than one and half feet long. I guess he had broken his putter and had to putt one-handed. Several members had come out to watch the match and surely wondered what was going on. Finally, Bobby missed about a two-foot putt and the match was over. On the ride back to the clubhouse, Bobby's dad took that putter and broke what was left of it in half.

I got my first taste of statewide junior competition at thirteen when I played in my first Texas Junior Amateur Championship at Brackenridge Park in San Antonio. I shot 70 in qualifying and wound up in the championship flight with boys up to eighteen years old. I made it to the quarterfinals, where Terry McMichael from a tiny town called Daingerfield beat me on the eighteenth hole.

The following year I discovered girls and, not coincidentally, didn't qualify for the tournament. I admit I spent a lot of time with Margaret Kreisle, but when I missed the qualifying Dad put it another way.

"You left a lot of golf in that girl's living room," he said.

I don't doubt that. Ironically, I was seeing Margaret off to camp that summer on August 1 when Austin came to a standstill as Charles Whitman opened fire from atop the University of Texas tower, killing fourteen people and injuring dozens more. As a merchant on The Drag—Guadalupe Street, which borders the campus on the west side—said, putting Whitman's ninety-six-minute shooting spree into perspective, "He was our initiation into a terrible time."

It hit home with our family for so many reasons, primarily because Bonnie was working on her masters in library science that summer and studied in the stacks inside the Tower and usually walked across the Main Mall about noon—just about the time Whitman was shooting. Fortunately she had stayed home that morning to study for a final. We watched it unfold on television, but Charlie, being your basic teenager, snuck out with Edward White, drove to the campus, and watched from the top of then-Memorial Stadium. It wasn't the smartest thing to do because even that was within Whitman's range, but he didn't fire in Charlie's direction.

I staged a big comeback in 1967, beating Wayne Fenack of Brownsville in the finals, which was a big deal because the event always produced a good winner. I love Brackenridge Park, a Tillinghast course once home to the Texas Open, where Mike Souchak set an all-time PGA Tour scoring record of twenty-seven-under-par 257 in 1955. Back then we were required to play our tee shots off of rubber mats, and we felt we could hit it a mile provided we could keep our shot down the narrow fairways. And, we always stopped at the sandwich stand just past the twelfth hole, where two old ladies would serve you the best sandwiches and lemonade in the world under the shade of the big oaks and pecan trees. Terry Jastrow, an excellent player from Midland who later produced golf for ABC Sports and is now head of Jack Nicklaus Productions, won in 1966, and Bruce Lietzke won the year I skipped.

I was really excited when I qualified for the U.S. Junior Amateur. Dad had already given me Charlie Price's book and I had read a little blurb in *Golf World* that the tournament was going to be held at Brookline the next year. When Dad told me we'd go if I qualified, I started right then and there conjuring up all sorts of images of Brookline. After all, with the exception of that trip to St. Louis and a trip or two to Alabama where Dad grew up, I had never seen many places outside Texas.

My world was about to open up, and my affair and those unbelievable ties with The Country Club were about to begin.

Dad and I flew up there on Braniff Airlines, stayed at a motel near the course, and just had the best time. In the space of two days we went to a Red Sox game at Fenway Park, where I soaked up the chance to see the green monster and the hand-controlled scoreboard; we walked the

Freedom Trail, saw Old North Church, got lost coming back from Fenway with a kid from Cincinnati—Casey Krug and his dad—and I got my first look at The Country Club.

Getting lost in Boston is easy. Everyone does it. I always chuckle over Lee Trevino's description of that city—"You fly into the airport, you go through a few tunnels, get lost four or five times, go through some more tunnels, then you finally get to a golf course." That's pretty much the way it is. At least while we were driving aimlessly we somehow wound up at The Country Club, and we knew how to get to the hotel from there.

My first impression of the club was how stately it was. The clubhouse was so charming, the colors were so vibrant, and I'd never seen trees that tall in my life. It was a montage of New England.

It was my first national tournament and I'd done my homework, reading little snippets in *Golf Digest* and *Golf World* about guys like Eddie Pearce, Gary Koch, and Billy Harmon. But this was my first time to meet them. There was a big pool of young talent up there.

Billy, the youngest son of 1948 Masters champion Claude Harmon, was one of the most highly touted players. I went over to him and nervously introduced myself as he was hitting bunker shots by the practice green. He didn't know me from Adam and really didn't know what to say, so I just stood there and thought to myself what a good-looking player he was. We got past that awkward moment and I've been friends with him and his brothers—Butch, who watches over Tiger Woods' swing; Dick, the pro at River Oaks Country Club in Houston; and Craig, the pro at Oak Hill Country Club in Rochester, N.Y.—for decades now.

Eddie Pearce was the best junior player in the country and was touted as the next star in golf, but he lost confidence in his putting after college and has struggled ever since. And Gary, who eventually played at Florida, was low qualifier that week. I already knew Bruce Lietzke, whom I'd competed against in Texas and who would become one of my closest friends and an assistant captain for me in 1999, but I also met the likes of Bill Kratzert, David Eger, and Bobby Wadkins.

I saw some good golf up there and I played some good golf, easing through the two qualifying rounds and beating David Eger in the first round. Eventually I got beat in the quarterfinals by the New Orleans junior champion, Larry Griffin, on the eighteenth hole. He had a slightly unorthodox swing, but he knew it well. So well that he hit an 8-iron six feet from the hole on that final hole to beat me. It was a tough pill to swallow, but I came away knowing I could play with those guys.

After I was eliminated we stayed on and watched Bruce, who lost to Eddie in the semifinals. Eddie then beat Bill Harman from Wilmington, Delaware, in the finals. To this day Eddie remains one of the most talented players I have ever seen. He possessed a swing like Sam Snead's, a beautiful shoulder turn with lots of power, and he was reaching the par fives easily, which most of the other juniors couldn't do. He was magic. Sadly, that magic just didn't last.

I soaked in a ton of golf that week. It was the first time I had ever seen people follow a match in coats and ties—Boston was so proper—and I stared in amazement at the terrain and the beautiful bent-grass fairways. I was scared to take a divot because the grass just looked too beautiful. I finally overcame that, and can remember thinking it was such an interesting course with its smallish greens and granite outcroppings.

The trip made a lasting impression on me. In one wondrous week, golf history, architecture, and big-time competition hit me over the head. Even though I didn't win, I grew up a lot. The Country Club was, for me, the Fountainhead. I didn't realize it then, but Brookline would play such a big part in my career. Bigger than I could ever have imagined.

4.

A FRIENDSHIP AND
A RIVALRY

BEST JUNIOR PLAYERS I'VE
PLAYED AGAINST

Eddie Pearce
Tom Kite
Joe Anderson
Bruce Lietzke
Lester Lundell
Gary Koch

The picture was taken when we were shooting scenes for Harvey's "The Little Green Video" out at Austin Country Club. There's Harvey sitting on his cart on the driving range, sandwiched by me and Tom Kite. I'm fiddling with a club on one side; Tom's watching and talking from the other.

As I look at it, so many memories come flooding back. Decades of stories. So many moments. Yet here we are—Tom and I are in our forties—together with Harvey on a driving range for one of the few times in our careers. Three men from the same city whose lives will be forever entwined. Three men who meant so much to each other.

Two men who wouldn't be who they are today without the older one.

Harvey never would let Tom or me see him working with the other one. He purposely kept us apart, nurturing each of our games in his own special way. It always seemed strange that we never worked with him at the same time, but that defines the beauty of Harvey's teaching and the knowledge he possessed in attempting to handle us both. I finally understood it when we both became professionals. He had to treat us differently because we were such different people.

Over the years we've been very good for each other in a way that drove us both. And it all started one hot afternoon as Charlie and I were finishing up the back nine at Austin Country Club.

As we walked through the parking lot in our cutoffs and T-shirts we saw a boy about our age dressed in slacks and carrying this big, red leather Wilson bag that looked like one a pro would carry. He had red hair, glasses, and was dressed like a little professional. We introduced ourselves and he said, "Y'all mind if I play the back nine with you?"

Charlie and I looked at him, gave him the once over, then said, sure, it would be okay. On the tenth tee Charlie and I couldn't help noticing three things—that big red bag, a brand new set of men's Wilson staff clubs, and brand new black-and-white Etonic golf shoes. We couldn't believe it. We were juniors, kids eleven and twelve, in cutoffs and sweaty shirts carrying little bags filled with what all kids played with back then—a ragtag assortment of ladies' and junior clubs. The kind everyone we knew learned with.

Charlie and I teed off, then Tom stepped to the tee with a driver that was obviously too long for him. He took a big swing, hit the ground about two feet behind the ball, and his clubhead just bounced right over the ball. Charlie and I stared at each other in amazement. We didn't know what to say. Obviously this was his first round with those clubs.

His next swing was pretty good though, and by the end of nine holes Charlie and I could tell that he could really play. I suppose we should have known he was destined to be a U.S. Open champion just by the way he looked when we saw him that day. He was two years older than me and had just moved to Austin from Dallas. Little did we know then that he and I would soon be mentioned constantly in the same breath, just like a cheeseburger and fries.

Because of that two-year difference we only played against each other one year in high school—I was a sophomore at Austin High; he was a senior at McCallum—but the comparisons were always there. We were very different players—he was into the mechanics of the swing and I played by feel—but we're both Texans. We both played junior golf in Austin. We both went to the University of Texas and shared the NCAA individual title in 1972. We both turned pro within a year of each other—Tom in 1972 and me in 1973—and we both won majors. I followed him as Ryder Cup captain.

After I won my second Masters, Tom sent me an intensely personal letter that meant more to me than I can explain. We had helped see each other through Harvey's death—returning to Austin together with our wives for the funeral in the middle of that Masters week—and he put that letter in the context of the time it was happening and how we both felt.

It was very complimentary about how I played and how I stood through the week. He talked about Harvey and how so much of our lives will always be intertwined with his. It threaded how far we've both come in the game, by each other, for our parents, and with Harvey. It was a beautiful letter and extremely meaningful. It didn't have any connotation of burying any hatchets because there weren't any. It's just something understood between us. All that talk of a rivalry is a misnomer. People have tried to create one, but it never existed. We are different people. But we're friends.

He is everything I'm not. He's absolutely organized, consistent, and concise. His aims are extremely clear and he works to achieve those goals in a structured manner that is wholly lacking with me. We've realized that forever. Tom writing me after that Masters . . . all I can say is that it was as meaningful to me as I hope the letter I wrote to Tom after his U.S. Open win at Pebble Beach in 1992 was to him. It's a very deep, personal, mutual respect we have for each other and it's truly amazing. If that victory at the Open is the only non-Senior Tour major he ever wins, I think of how appropriate it is that it happened at Pebble Beach—a course that means so much to him—and in such tough conditions.

While most of the field was taking steps back on that gale-like Sunday, Tom ground out an even-par 72. That shows what kind of player he is and why he won nineteen times on the PGA Tour. He's been so consistent, something that I could never manage. He played on seven Ryder Cup teams, won two Vardon Trophies for low scoring average, was the first player in history to reach the six-million, seven-million, eight-million, and nine-million-dollar marks in career earnings, and was the Tour's leading money winner twice, in 1981 and 1989. That's a terrific record.

As close as we are though, there are some real differences. Tom knows more about his game, mechanically, than just about anyone. On the other hand, I am a "feel" player. My game is based on instinct, and I know what works for me. That's part of the reason why Harvey would spend more time with Tom on the practice tee while sending me out to play the course.

And, I was much more the kid who would play eighteen, go for a swim, and play eighteen more. Tom spent his extra time on the driving range. Of course, there may have been something to say for that, especially when I look back to high school—back to the worst and longest day and a half of my life.

It all started one night when Jake White, whose father was former Democratic national chairman John C. White, and I got his older brother to buy us a twelve-pack of Schlitz Tall Boy Malt Liquor. We must have been about sixteen, and we had just iced it down and put it in the trunk when a cop pulled up. Jake tried to run, but the policeman told us to open the trunk.

"What are y'all gonna do with this?" he inquired.

For some reason Jake blurted out, "Oh, we just found it."

The cop looked at us and said, "Okay. Get in the car and follow me to the police station."

My parents and Jake's had to come and get us. We didn't get home until 12:30 that night, and there wasn't a word spoken on the way back from the police station. And to make things worse I had to pick up all the Austin High golf team the next morning at 6:30 to go to Brady.

Dad walked to the door of the bedroom I shared with Charlie, and the last thing I heard as he closed the door was, "Son, it was just like someone sticking a knife in my back."

I was lying there crying, and two minutes later Charlie got the nerve to ask, "God, you idiot. *What* did you do?"

Of course I was late picking everyone up the next morning, so we really had to hurry. I was speeding in that 1965 Cutlass Coupe— Charlie's and my first car—and when we screeched up to the clubhouse five minutes before our tee time the car's engine was smoking. Our coach, Milton O'Dell, was waiting for us, and a guy who played on the Johnston High team and knew something about cars screamed, "Don't turn it off! Don't turn it off! You'll blow the engine!"

Of course I did, and it went *boom*!

We played—I shot 66—and on our way home a guy at a gas station told us I'd melted the engine. He gave us four quarts of oil and warned me not to go over thirty-five miles an hour, so it took us forever to get back to Austin. Every time I stepped on the accelerator, the exhaust belched huge plumes of white smoke. Needless to say, Charlie and my parents were severely, severely disappointed. We drove Mom's car for a while after that, then Dad got us this Buick 455 Grand Sport, the hottest car ever. We couldn't believe it. God, it was a fast car. I think my Dad had a very weak moment when he bought that for us.

I was driving that car, in fact, the first day Brent Buckman, one of my soon-to-be Texas teammates, saw me for the first time. I was, of course, late for my high school match at Morris Williams Golf Course and I squealed into the parking lot again, jumped out of the car, hit my tee shot, and put my shoes on as I walked down the first fairway. I made my tee time and I didn't blow up the car. Amazing.

When the time came to choose a college, I wasn't really serious about any school but Texas. I did think about SMU because my girlfriend at the time, Nancy Hager, lived in Dallas, and there were a lot of fine courses in that area. I also thought briefly about Houston because Dave Williams had such a good program there. But when the time came, I knew I belonged at Texas.

Coach Royal, whose UT Longhorns had just won the national college football championship following a 15–14 win over Arkansas, was there when I signed, and that meant a lot to Dad. It was clearly another fortunate decision I made. It really was. Texas had a good program with George Hannon, who took over when Harvey retired, and the university itself is a network of people. There was something about the vastness that captivated us all, but there was also such a legacy. People going in step back and say, "This is daunting. I have a lot to live up to."

Tom and I shared the top spot most of the two years we were together. I was fortunate enough to win the individual title all three years—sharing the second with Tom—and we won the team title my first two years. During that time we had a great rivalry with Houston, where Bruce Lietzke, Bill Rogers, and Jim McLean all played. That was where we formed friendships that would last forever. Bill—we call him Buck—and Lietzke—he's Leaky—were my assistants at the Ryder Cup. Tom was in Brookline and made it a point to come by and support the team. Jim dropped by, too. We knew each other so well as players and as teams, we were never sure who was going to win when we teed it up.

And when we beat them by one shot one year at the Border Olympics? Dave Williams was so upset, they all piled into that old station wagon Dave drove and headed for Houston. Not a word was spoken for forty or fifty miles. Everyone was too scared to speak.

Buck was in the front riding shotgun and Dave finally looked over. "Texarkana, Texarkana," he said, since he referred to players not by their names, but what cities they were from, plus he always repeated himself. "Look in that glove compartment there and see if there's a gun in there. I think I'm just going to shoot myself."

Another time he went ballistic and told the team that if anyone ever repeated the names of Texas players—especially Kite or Crenshaw—again, they wouldn't play for him again.

See, Kite and Crenshaw. Crenshaw and Kite. We'd played against each other in the City Men's Championships as kids, but people really took notice when we played for Texas. And it was strange that it would come down between us for the 1972 NCAA individual title.

Tom led after two days and, with Texas having won the year before, all of us were keeping our eyes on the team race. I don't remember exactly when it was, but someone came up and told us we couldn't lose the team title. Then, someone told me I had to par the last hole to tie Tom for medalist.

Having heard that, I made the most desperate par you can imagine. After hitting my drive behind a tree, I chipped out and was about twenty yards in front of the green. I chipped that up and left myself with a twenty-foot uphill putt on a terribly grainy green. I knew I had to strike it hard, but I hit it so hard it bounced off the back of the hole, flew up, and fell right into the cup.

Everyone was watching but Tom. He was lying down beside the green, afraid to watch. Afterward we thought we were going into a playoff when a guy came up and declared us co-champions. All we could think was, how could this be? We were bewildered. We wanted to have a playoff. Of course, that could have been yet another playoff loss in my career, where I'm horrible—0-for-8 on the PGA Tour.

Tom and I are proud of our achievements and each other's. We have different circles of friends and live in different areas of Austin, but we've always been there for each other—and to push each other. Now we're pushing each other on the Senior Tour.

5.

LITTLE BEN

BEST PUTTERS

Billy Casper
Jack Nicklaus
Bobby Locke
Bobby Jones
George Archer
Tiger Woods
Tom Watson
Phil Mickelson
Loren Roberts

He was sitting with a few of his brothers in a rack at Muny, a fifteen-dollar price tag taped underneath the grip. I picked him up and let my fingers curl around the grip. I'd been putting—and winning—with an old Bullseye, but this club just somehow seemed special. I put him back alongside his siblings, a handful of Wilson 8802 putters that were just a bit heavier and a shade darker.

I didn't really need a new putter, but that wasn't the point. I was sixteen now, back from the U.S. Junior Amateur and on my way—to where, I wasn't sure. I needed clubs I could depend on and this putter looked good in my hands. It felt pretty good, too. And, without the least bit of urging—that may have been a first in my young life—Dad brought it home one night and handed it to me.

Give or take two abductions, a few stints on the bench, and some repair time on a worktable or two, Little Ben hasn't left my side. And even when he has been banished from the lineup for bad behavior, he still finds his way into the bag for, if nothing else, moral support.

Invariably I take him to the True Temper truck near the driving range, and the guys down there just shake their heads. Dave Rennie, one of the guys there, calls it "the putter from hell." He hates to see it coming because he knows he'll have to do something to it.

It may sound strange to have such an attachment to a club, but I do. He's been a great, great friend over the years and my longest-lasting relationship other than my family, Harvey, and longtime friends like Scotty Sayers and Bobby Kay. We've been to hell and back. We've won a Masters and nineteen other professional events around the world (he wasn't present for two of my wins). We've both been broken, bent, and twisted; we've had incredible highs and inconsolable lows, but we've always bounced back.

He's like Willie Nelson's guitar. It's old, beat-up, and doesn't look like it's worth a darn, but it's something that feels right to Willie and he doesn't care what that old guitar looks like. When I asked him why he kept it, he said simply, "It's feel. I've tried a lot of others, but you go back to what feels good."

That's me and Little Ben.

He got his name, by the way, from Dad. Dad loved names like the ones Bobby Jones had for his clubs—Calamity Jane, Jeannie Deans. And one day he called my putter Little Ben. It was an innocent name and it stuck. Everyone asks about him. He may be the best-known putter this side of Calamity Jane, but all I know is I owe a lot to him.

Throughout my professional career I had to lean on that putter hard to bail me out. There's no question it did some extraordinary things. The times when I played well, it served me well, but the times I didn't play well, it helped me hang on. I'll never forget going through good, long stretches where I expected to make three thirty-footers every day. When people talk these days about a round of golf not being a good round unless you have thirty or less putts, well, Little Ben and I were there for a good long while. That's what held me together when I wasn't hitting the ball well and it shows the power of the short game.

Every time I think about the times he's left my hands for no apparent reason or the times I've kicked him, or tossed him at the bag or up a tree, and—in two cases—snapped his shaft, I see Dave Marr shaking his head at me.

"We're going to get you for child abuse," he would say. "You're always chastising Little Ben. You have treated him so poorly."

I have.

He still bears the scars.

New putters always had a certain glare to them and so did this one. One club member had a similar putter—an Arnold Palmer model— that he had doctored with black tape to kill the shine. I wasn't about to do that. Instead, I got the bright idea to take a file and file that chrome off of him. After filing about two and a half inches away, I got tired and quit. And I left it that way—with the ragged edges of the exposed metal making it look worn and much older than its thirty-four or so years.

I look at him now—he also has a spike mark on the flange where I stepped on him by accident one day that now serves as a guideline for a downhill, a really fast putt that I have to hit on the toe to get a more dead hit—and he reflects the state of my golf game at age fifty. He's worn and tired, and he's been all over the world with me many times, but right now he's on life support. Oh, he still has life left in him and he's made the trip to the Senior Tour with me. I have that much affection for him. I just wish he had the same feel.

Little Ben hasn't been the same since that final day at the 1987 Ryder Cup at Muirfield Village when, after three-putting the sixth green, I walked off holding the putter-head in my hand. Why I don't know. I never carry him like that. I usually hold him by the shaft.

Anyway, I walked off the edge of the green and took about ten steps toward the seventh tee, and there was a buckeye on the ground—one of those big ol' nuts. Swinging for the buckeye, I hit the shaft on the ground instead and snapped it in two. All I could think was "Omigod. What a time for this to happen."

I was shocked. I was in trouble off the seventh tee and conceded that hole, so I didn't putt there, but just as I was going up the steps to the eighth tee I met Jack Nicklaus, our captain.

"How are things going back there?" he asked.

"Pretty good," I said, trying my best to mumble. "ButIbrokemy-putterbackthere."

He heard it and looked at me with those eyes. "You did what?"

"I broke my putter," I said, hanging my head.

"Oh God," he said, shaking his. "Well, the way things are going, I don't blame you. Just do the best you can."

I putted in with either my sand wedge or my 1-iron the rest of the way and Eamonn Darcy actually conceded a three and a half footer at the eighth hole. At the time, he didn't know my putter was broken. I lost the last two holes to lose 1-up, and, a year later, I realized that Eamonn still didn't know about the putter. He came up to me at the British Open and told me he thought I had shelved the putter in favor of the other clubs to try and slow the ball down on the greens because they were so fast.

"No, Eamonn," I said chuckling. "I'm not that good."

Ironically, the shaft that broke had been in Little Ben since the year after I got him. His first shaft met a violent end in one of two ways—and I honestly can't remember which. Either I laid my bag down, threw another club at it, and hit the putter in exactly the right spot and snapped it, or I threw him and he snapped. What I do remember is that Hiram Elliott, the father of Bob Elliott, the pro at Northwood Country Club in Dallas, worked on clubs and reshafted and regripped him so well that the job lasted until that Ryder Cup.

I've tried probably twenty-five different shafts in there since and haven't been able to duplicate the feel that I once had. I even had Scotty take him to Austin jeweler Phil Shaw, who soldered the shaft together with a little silver band and it enjoined the two parts—and I've still got it. I used it at the Tour Championship at Oak Hill in 1987 and tied for fifth, but it was only a Band-Aid and wasn't enough. I know it sounds crazy, but putting is all about feel. It's ridiculous, but I just never have been able to get that feel back.

Little Ben has always been a putter that's fit me. With that old shaft, it swung right, it looked right, and I think the weight of it helped me on slow and fast greens. People amuse themselves about it—and it is over the top—but I'm not the only one. Jack had that 3-wood of his that he used forever because it was perfect for him. He got it in 1958 and didn't stop using it until 1995. I'm sure that people kidded him about that club, too.

What's ironic is that everyone talks about my feel and my putting, but Harvey always said I was an average putter. When I was growing up—say, age fifteen through college—I could really hit the ball well. And despite hearing players like Tom Kite and Buck Rogers say they never saw me miss a putt when I was an amateur, hitting was easier for me and progressed a lot quicker than my skill on the greens.

In fact, the best ball-striking round I ever had was when I won the Firecracker Open—Austin's big Fourth of July tournament at Muny—in 1969. During one four-hole stretch I either drove or just narrowly missed the green on three 350-yard-plus par fours and started the streak by reaching a long par five with a driver and 5-iron. I shot 64 that day. It was an amazing stretch.

I guess I started really holing putts in college, but it wasn't until my second or third year on tour that I realized how important my putting was. When I would not play well but still come up with a decent score, I figured it out. And, learning to putt at so many different places around the world and on so many different types of greens helped, too. I learned right then and there, no matter where you play, you have to get the ball in the hole.

That's one thing that amazes me about Tiger Woods. I have such a great time watching him putt. I know people love to watch him hit the ball—and just love watching him, period—but I hope they understand that they really, really, really need to watch his short game.

Some writers understand it and have written about it, but I have to tell you that his Masters win in 1997 was absolutely beautiful on the greens. Tiger did not miss anything six feet and under. He didn't three-putt; he didn't miss a crucial putt all week. The way he putted relaxed him enough that he could do anything.

His stroke is very authoritative, which it should be at his age. Every player under twenty-eight or so feels that way, but his stroke is also so mechanically sound. It's solid, simple, and very, very pure. He does exactly what Harvey told me—Be yourself. Try not to stand there and pretend you're someone else.

When I think about that week I see a small montage of all the putts that rolled into holes at every juncture. And if you don't think that doesn't give you confidence . . .

Tiger aside, Jack was one of the consistently fine putters who played the game. His approach putting was absolutely incredible. No matter where he was, he'd hit it up there within one and a half feet. No strain at all on a second putt. Then he would seemingly always make the important putts whether they were for par or birdie—no matter what tournament it was.

Little Ben was with me for that first Masters win, sinking that sixty-footer on the tenth hole in the final round, but he was on the shelf in 1995, replaced by a Ben Crenshaw–designed Cleveland Classics putter that belonged to my manager Scotty. My wife Julie nicknamed him Little Scotty that week and he performed just like Little Ben had in 1984.

The only other win I had without Little Ben was at the 1992

Western Open, but it wasn't because he was misbehaving. It was because he'd been stolen—for the second time in his life.

His first abduction was in 1990. I was flying home from the Doral Ryder Open and was connecting through Atlanta. During the baggage transfer a part-time Delta employee took him out of my bag. At the time he had a blue paddle grip, and another employee recognized him and said, "You can't be selling that club." That guy told Tour player Bob Lohr and Bob put him in touch with me. The guy then flew Little Ben to Houston, where I was about to play in the Houston Open, and Julie and I went to the airport to get him. A few weeks later he and I won our second Colonial title in Fort Worth.

The second theft came on a rainy night in Austin. I had left my car unlocked in our driveway and someone broke into the car and stole the whole Cleveland Classics bag. I was beside myself and Julie even tacked "stolen/reward" flyers on poles in our neighborhood. About three weeks later someone spotted them in the back of a car at a drive-in liquor store in San Marcos, about thirty minutes south of Austin. I eventually got the entire set of clubs and the bag back, but not until after I'd won the Western Open using a different Cleveland putter—but one similar to the 8802—than the one I used to win the Masters.

That broken shaft wasn't the only problem Little Ben and I encountered in the late 1980s. Just about that same time the USGA banned the grip that I—and a lot of other players like Dave Stockton, Nancy Lopez, and George Archer—had been using, the Golf Pride paddle grip. Little Ben's original grip was a leather one with a silver band, but when Mr. Elliott reshafted him, he also regripped him with one of those paddle grips. And I putted with that until the USGA deemed it illegal in 1988.

Actually, Frank Hannigan, former USGA executive director, gave me a heads-up on the upcoming ruling when I was playing in the 1987 U.S. Open at Olympic Club.

I don't want to bore you with this, but I think it's a travesty that you can't use this grip. I putted with this grip for almost twenty years and—all of a sudden—it became illegal? Countless people have putted with this grip, but the USGA and Royal and Ancient recodified the book—condensed the rule book—and suddenly said a grip cannot have a bulge or a waist in it, and it cannot be molded for the hand.

I'm absolutely perplexed by it, so much so that I've written them and talked with them several times. I've never been satisfied with their answers.

The rule book also says the grip must be plain in shape, and the paddle is as straight as any on the market. Now you talk about a Ping grip or some of these others and they have curves in them like a curved toothbrush. The paddle grip is straighter and plainer in form than a lot of "legal" grips on the market. To me, the language in the rule book is ambiguous.

I want to know why a person would putt better with it. It's a matter of feel to me. People say, why can't you putt with something similar? Because I putted with this for twenty-five years and nothing feels better to me. I know it's personal. I know it's quirky the way that I look at it, but it's what my feel is based on. And a lot of companies have tried to replicate this grip to conform to the rules, but it's just not the same.

In the same vein, to approve the long putter and disallow this grip differs from the regulation method. The way I put it in a letter to the USGA is "at least I have a free expression of the stroke." Nothing but my hands touch the club. Another part of my body does not. Whether people rest it against their chin, or whether they stick it in their chest or sternum or stomach, this is not a free expression. You go back and see what the USGA has disallowed in the past—the croquet style, even the center-shafted Schenectady putter which the R&A banned because Walter Travis happened to make a bunch of putts and win the British Amateur in 1904. When he did, they said, well, that club can't be legal. He made too many putts.

Now a large numbers of players around the world are putting with the long putter. Even young players are picking it up.

My thoughts are strictly my opinion. They've disallowed a lot of things in the past, but rulings by the balls and implement committee are both scientific and subjective matters. It's very difficult to know where to draw the line, but I do agree that there needs to be an authority in concert with the R&A.

I believe that in the heavy majority of cases they've done what's right for the game. There are always going to be detractors—like me—in certain situations like these with putters and technology. What I don't like about the golf ball and the length of clubs is where course architecture has to go. I don't think it's good to stretch out courses to 7,300 or 7,400 yards to counter the length. To me it creates almost too much of a disparity between people who play in competitions, people who play on a regular basis, and recreational players. An architect's job will always be to make a golf course that's playable for every class of golfer. It's easy to build a super-hard, diabolical test of golf—that's the easiest thing in the world. But I think we have reached what many others have termed a friction point.

It's not the first time golf has reached one of these points and won't be the last. The first one came around 1870 when the feather ball gave way to the gutta-percha ball. That's when old Tom Morris left St. Andrews over the matter and went to Prestwick for twelve years, because he and Allan Robertson, who was still a feather ball maker, had a disagreement as to where the game was going.

Another point was right around the turn of the century when the rubber-core golf ball was introduced. Obviously that did much to provide a mass appeal for the game, but there were a lot of detractors. Then, more controversy flared up when the hickory shaft went out in the '20s and was replaced by steel. The latest flap has been over metal woods.

Now it's technology, period. I do feel a little despondent that some of the old courses are beginning to be classified as outdated—some are the best courses ever built. Merion is a vibrant example. A majority of players can come close to overpowering that course now.

Jack Nicklaus has been talking about it for twelve or fourteen years. He's been watching the golf ball and was one of the early proponents of a regulation ball. And whether you agree with him or not, it's time to think about it.

But the age-old argument in golf is always going to be between the manufacturers and the ruling bodies. They've not always peacefully coexisted and there's not a scenario in which they can. I suppose if you drew a line in the sand—for most instances—ruling bodies have done an extremely sensible job. It's truly a case where you can't make everyone happy. And their job is to protect the integrity of the game, which covers a lot of ground because it encompasses everything a golfer does—etiquette, rules, competitions, what people expect of future generations. Golf is probably *the* most traditional game around. It's tough to govern a game that's been around for five hundred years, and although the first set of rules wasn't drafted until 1744, they've done pretty well.

I would just like to see sensible limits, but they're very hard to legislate. Who'd have ever thought of the idea of pushing back six or eight of the tee boxes at St. Andrews? It's not just Tiger that's forcing this. I don't want to lament the loss of the old days—it's not that. But just try to think about all the golfers who play around the world, and it's happening everywhere. If the USGA does think technology inherently changes the game, I hope they'll act. And, honestly, I think we're approaching that.

Having said all that, I guess I just wish I had Little Ben back the way he was—the perfect shaft, the paddle grip, the feel that I had with him for so many years. I think back to that Masters. To a fifty-footer and a forty-footer I made in the final round in 1976 to win the Hawaiian Open. To the twenty-footer at the NCAAs. To the putt I made to win at Doral in 1988.

Little Ben? He's just part of me. If I couldn't putt, there's no telling what path my career would have taken. I've putted very well over the years, but no better than Tom Watson, Billy Casper, or Bobby Locke.

And, I've come a long way from the average putter Harvey knew. I owe a lot of it to Little Ben.

6.

GENTLE BEN

MOST VOLATILE PLAYERS

Bobby Jones
Tommy Bolt
Tom Weiskopf
Jackie Burke
Lefty Stackhouse
Dave Hill
Steve Pate

It wasn't anyplace special. Not a place to take a date or anyone you wanted to impress. Just a smoky dive where you could shoot pool, play table shuffleboard, sample Pee-Wee's famous nachos, fried oysters, or chicken fried steak, and—if you happened to be underage—sip a beer or two with no one asking you for an ID.

You're naturally going to gravitate to a place like that, where you knew for a short while, at least, they'd serve you as a minor. And you're going to have a soft spot in your heart for it—even after it's been gone for fifteen years.

That's me and Jake's.

I can't drive past that empty lot on Fifth Street without thinking about those afternoons and nights when we'd hang out and play shuffleboard on the old wooden table. That table is at Shoal Creek Saloon now and, I'll tell you, the people playing on it know there's a lot of local knowledge involved. It was raised on one side you had to know what you were doing to be any good on it. And if someone gave Pee Wee, the proprietor, trouble about anything, he knew how to fix him. He'd go pull the plug on the air conditioner so when the troublemaker threw the puck down there it would skid to a stop because the table had so much humidity on it.

I remember one night when a guy with extremely long hair complained about Pee Wee's french fries. Pee Wee, whose bathroom signs read "pointers" and "setters," got him by the pants and tossed him out. "In forty years, no one's complained about my fries," he said. "I'm not going to serve you."

They didn't much like long hair there and, in college, my hair flipped up over my collar, just like everyone else's. They'd tease me about being a hippie and getting a haircut, but I never did.

My appearance was deceiving. So was my nickname.

Sometime back then, Austin sportswriter Dick Collins nicknamed me Gentle Ben and it stuck. Everyone always assumed he got it from the television show by that name starring Clint Howard and a bear named Gentle Ben. I never understood what Dick was thinking. I guess he saw it as a takeoff on Jack's nickname, Golden Bear. Plus, this bear on the television show was playful and wouldn't hurt anybody. And neither would I.

You know about my love for birds, but what you don't know is I cry at movies like *Beauty and the Beast* and *Lonesome Dove*. And, I won't even kill a tarantula. Once when one was loose in the house Julie wanted me to kill it. I caught it in a jar and set it free near a creek.

But Dick didn't know all those things. What he did know was that I had a temper and that Dad was always getting after me. So, as I just recently learned, the nickname had nothing to do with that show. It was actually a sarcastic jab at my hot temper. Dick saw it often, put his tongue in his cheek one day, and came up with the nickname Gentle Ben.

It stuck.

My friends have always found it amusing since they know the real me—the one who cries and tries to be nice to everyone; the one who beats himself up a lot. And when I do get upset I throw clubs, I break clubs, and, at least once, I broke some bones.

It was at the 1980 Colonial National Invitation. I had myself in contention, but I three-putted the par-three sixteenth. It was stupid and I got so mad I walked off the green and kicked an oil drum trash can with my right foot.

I paid the price for years.

The next day I was limping and had to cut the top out of my shoe and told Jerry McGee, my playing partner, about it. "Oh, I've done that a million times," he said.

Just not with such disastrous results.

It turned out that I had fractured the sesamoid bone on the bottom of the foot, but it didn't show up until years later when the toe got arthritic and I could hardly walk on it. Finally in 1997 I had surgery to remove that bone and shave down a big calcium deposit in a joint on my big toe that resulted from the injury.

That's where Gentle Ben and the Real Ben sort of cross paths in reality. The notion that I was actually some sort of placid wallflower is a misnomer. I wasn't much different than a lot of players who got hot and threw clubs and kicked things, and because of it I see the humor in the nickname, absolutely. That probably makes it better, really.

But that wasn't any consolation one year when Mom came out to Morris Williams Golf Course to watch me in a college tournament. I was teeing off on the seventeenth hole and pushed the ball to the right. I took my driver—a Jack Nicklaus model I loved—and banged it against the tee marker, breaking it.

"Oh, Bennie," Mom said, sounding very ashamed.

I felt horrible. The pity in her voice and the pain in her face really hurt. I was so embarrassed, so ashamed.

Over the years I broke a lot of clubs. Maybe more than most, maybe not. But Dad made me pay for them. A shaft would cost me a dollar or something back then, but I would scrounge up the money from my brother to pay for a new shaft. You would think I'd learn, but I didn't.

Harvey knew that I threw clubs, too, because he would hear it from a lot of people. He never said much about it, but he did say a little temper is going to show through sometimes. "If you don't have a temper, you are not going anywhere," he said. But that was a statement, not a defense.

Temper always has been an issue. Today people get mad at Tiger all the time for his temper, but he is a real competitor. He just gets upset with himself sometimes. You have to learn how to bottle it and he's managed to do that. It's just that everything he does is magnified. Like that tee shot on eighteen at the 2000 U.S. Open at Pebble Beach.

I imagine he was fined for that because a lot of players have been fined for doing that same thing over the years. I got fined five hundred dollars for throwing a club at my bag at the 1983 Open at Oakmont. I tossed my club at my bag, the official saw me, and I think the fine came for a "moving club violation."

Almost all players are tough on themselves like that. The one regret I have is that I was not good about letting little mistakes go. A shot I missed. A stupid bogey. They would stay with me for a few holes and that's not good. The times that I played well, I played better because I accepted mistakes.

One of the very best at blowing off steam and accepting mistakes was Arnold. He would blow his stack quickly and just get rid of the bad stuff. Seve Ballesteros used to say, "You just have to swallow it." And Jack was incredible, too. He would show a little disgust toward himself, but it never really got in the way of his thinking about the next shot. That's the trick. If you carry it over, it's going to hurt you. You can't stand over your next shot and give it your total concentration if you're still boiling about something you just messed up.

Just how much that held me back early in my pro career I'll never know. I had so many close calls in majors early on that I wonder what would have happened if I had been able to get over mistakes better. But I do know that the other side of the Gentle Ben tag did help me with the fans and the media when I did turn pro.

I have to admit I wasn't the greatest student. I did win three NCAA titles in a row and was fortunate enough to be given the Fred Haskins Award as the best golfer in the nation three times, too. So right then I started thinking about whether I was going to finish school. I started out in the business school, but that didn't last long and I sort of floated around the arts and sciences for a couple of years. Oh, I went to class. I had to. But . . .

My mind was on golf. I played in every important amateur tournament in the States and some around the world. If I wasn't playing for UT, chances are I was preparing for a U.S., a Western, or a Southern Amateur. And, in 1972, I was selected to the USGA's Eisenhower Cup team that played in Buenos Aires. Vinny Giles, Mark Hayes, Marty West, and I won despite our hotel—the Sheraton—being bombed one afternoon.

Yes, I was there. We all were. A bomb went off on the twenty-sixth floor—we were staying on the fifth floor—about 5 P.M. one afternoon and a Canadian woman was killed and lots of people were injured. Peronistas, an anti-American group, had planted several other bombs, which fortunately failed to detonate. If they had I wouldn't be telling this story today.

The State Department wanted us to come home because the group was celebrating Juan Perón's return from exile in Spain and they were targeting Americans in the city. But we stayed, won the tournament, and then got out of the country. Years later, when Julie asked me to go see *Evita*, I declined. I'd seen enough during that week in '72.

But back to the decision. I was about to finish my junior year when I had to decide whether to stay another year in school and play the Walker Cup at—yes—The Country Club in the fall, or turn pro. Think that wasn't a difficult decision? And there was Brookline, staring me straight in the face again. Anyway, it was a terribly painful decision not to play at Brookline on that Walker Cup team, but I decided to make that jump, to turn pro.

As you might imagine, my decision was a topic of discussion at home. Mom was always filled with soothing talk that everything would be fine. There weren't too many crises around my mother, the eternal optimist. My dad, on the other hand, was more of a pragmatist. He put things into perspective a little bit more and I could tell he wanted me to stay in school. He always wanted me to get a diploma. But he left it up to me.

I just thought the timing was right. I had played in two U.S. Opens (1970, 1971) and two Masters (1972, 1973) and made the cut all four times, even tying for nineteenth in my first Masters—the year Jack won his fourth jacket. My NCAA titles also allowed me—through special exemptions—to play in seven more PGA Tour events as an amateur and I made all eleven cuts. And, when I did turn pro, I was fortunate to get sponsors' exemptions into several fields.

In my first event—the USI Classic at Pleasant Valley—I tied for thirty-fifth and won $903. Then I played an event in Raleigh and finished twelfth—thanks to a 67 in the last round—and won $2,058. I followed that a few weeks later with a tie for eighth at the Sea Pines Heritage Classic, where I won $4,238.

So when I did go to the PGA Tour's qualifying school at Perdido Bay Country Club in Pensacola and the Dunes Club in Myrtle Beach, South Carolina, in the fall of 1973, I knew what to expect. And, after nearly missing the cut in the local qualifying at Las Colinas in Irving, I went to the final where I wound up as the medalist, winning Q-school over a field that included Gary McCord, Larry Nelson, and Gil Morgan by twelve shots.

That done, I made my official debut as a PGA Tour rookie at

Woodlake Country Club at the Texas Open. The Gentle Ben tag helped there as I drew a nice gallery, including a few coeds from Trinity University in San Antonio who wore T-shirts that read "Ben's Bunnies." Later I had another group following me—"Ben's Wrens."

Anyway, I couldn't believe I actually won that tournament. I was playing well and got wrapped up in trying to beat really established pros like Orville Moody, George Archer, and Mike Hill down the stretch. I played the last round with Orville, and I remember when we came up to the last hole I had a two-shot lead. Now, Orville was one of the straightest drivers I had ever seen. There was water on both sides of the fairway, and he took his driver, even though a lot of people were playing conservatively that week, and whipped it down the fairway between the lakes. He put pressure on me right there. But somehow I had the presence of mind to take out a 3-iron and I just hit it down the fairway, hit a good second shot, and a 9-iron into the green and—just like that—that was it. I shot 65-72-66-67 to beat Orville by two.

I'm probably proudest that I didn't take the bait when he challenged with that driver. He hit the most beautiful drive you ever saw, close to where he could get to the green in two and really put some pressure on me. But I played really well that week. And even better than winning was the $25,000 paycheck, which meant that Dad could pay off the bank loan he took out to help me.

Next up was an eight-round tournament at Pinehurst No. 2 and No. 4 called the World Open Golf Championship. Miller Barber won it, but I took home a very generous $44,175. To say that I was thrilled doesn't do it justice. To have that much in the bank after two weeks . . . you can't imagine the burden that lifted off me.

Actually I'd dug myself in even deeper during those two weeks. I was staying with Peter Tufts and his family—his grandfather had built Pinehurst—and I promised his teenage son Rick that if I won, I'd buy him a small motorcycle. So that second place actually saved me money.

At the same time the media had taken to me and I made the cover of *Sports Illustrated* when I was twenty-two. The story was written by Dan Jenkins, another Texan who just about invented modern-day sports-writing, and what he said about me was extremely flattering. I've kept the story all these years because of Dan's kind words:

"Charm, charisma, appeal. Some golfers have it built in, like a Palmer or a Lee Trevino, and others acquire it, as Nicklaus and Ben Hogan did, by winning. Crenshaw undoubtedly has it built in, Palmer style, but he appears to be starting out with even more golfing ability than Palmer had."

He had to be kidding, right?

And there was more: "In trying to explain why Crenshaw is already so popular, you have to start with how he looks. First of all, he is 22 but could pass for 17. This means he is a 'kid' out there with all those grownups. Crowds love a kid."

It still is so flattering to read that kind of story. And you see the backdrop "Gentle Ben" had when he started in the pros. A lot was expected of me. And I expected a lot, too.

So I was off and running, but the learning process, the mental part, was really in its infancy.

Over the past twenty-nine years I've developed sort of a theory about the pro golf mentality. Some of it involves ability, but if there is one thing that separates players on different levels, it's desire. Like Jimmy Demaret said: "You have to look around and if you can beat everybody in your town, then it is time to go look for different competition." But there is a vast difference between shooting good scores at home and shooting good scores when you take your game on the road.

Jimmy called golf a constant and endless and minute set of adjustments. From week to week, everything changes—and you do, too. You have to react to different grasses, textures of grasses, atmospheres, humidity, and everything related to weather and agronomy. You have to apply yourself to whatever you face and you have to change your game accordingly. You know that the greens may sit up a little more at a particular course and you may have to hit the ball a little bit higher. If you're playing at Augusta, you try to hit the ball as high as you can and to a certain spot because the greens are so firm. In Florida you keep the ball down because of the wind. Up north you hit the ball back up in the air again, and in California you know the courses play a lot longer than the yardage because you are close to the ocean. You just learn those things over time.

You know you'll hit the ball farther on desert courses and you'll know that in the heat of the day the ball is going to go a long way. In the cool mornings, though, you have to use more club.

It's enormous, the number of factors you must take into account and adapt to. As a junior or an amateur you're always fresh for a tournament. As a professional you play a lot more golf than ever before. You're earning your living and, instead of playing a dozen or so three-day college tournaments, now you're playing thirty weeks or more and having six-day work weeks.

Adapting isn't everything. A lot depends on what's in your head, too. The difference between winning and losing sometimes isn't that big. Those who can handle it best will enter a tight situation with confidence in their game, the right club in their hands, and the knowledge that they're going to make the right decision. That combination will get them through anything.

For instance, in the case of Hal Sutton and the 1983 PGA Championship at Riviera, he was absolutely dead-on and played beautiful golf that week. He played like a veteran, even though he was just twenty-five, leading wire-to-wire and beating Jack by a shot. That should give you a little indication of what Hal thought about his ability.

And Tiger Woods? He's one of the best I've ever seen mentally. He's displaying all the right traits now at such a young age and—this may be the understatement of all time—this portends well for his future. It's fascinating watching him play at such a high level. But he is succeeding because he is picturing these things in his mind. He talks about playing in the present and, man, does he do it. He never gets ahead of himself.

He's a mechanic, too, with his swing. He really knows it, and Butch Harmon has done an incredibly good job of helping him get to that point. You combine his mental discipline with that and his touch, his feel, and that's unique. It's a true gift. And his sense of the moment is spectacular. That's what he plays for and he thrives on it.

It's also what Jack was doing when he was at his best. They each had visions of themselves in that situation and knew if they did their job, they would succeed.

And you have to know the difference. Jimmy Demaret did when Mike Burke asked him what he thought about him turning pro. Jimmy knew no matter how many good shots Mike was hitting, he wasn't ready. So Jimmy took a deep breath and said, "Now, Mike, there are three guys who just came through this bar who can beat you." Mike got the point.

I'm not anything but realistic. And if there is anything this game has taught me, it's that sooner or later reality will pop you in the face, just as if you weren't watching and stepped on a bunker rake. I was always watching where I was stepping. I just wish I had known where the heck I was going.

I learned how to win a lot of regular Tour events, but for the longest time I couldn't figure out what it took to win a major. I'd get there but couldn't finish it off—starting in 1975 at the U.S. Open at Medinah.

I played very well in the first couple of rounds and was in the thick of things throughout the tournament, but my play was sort of desperate. I wasn't driving well, but I was scoring well. That last day, it was as if no one wanted to win. No less than six or seven players had a chance—Frank Beard, Jack, Lou Graham, Hale Irwin, John Mahaffey, Tom Watson, myself. I actually stood on the seventy-first tee, and I either had a one-shot lead or was tied, and knew that if I made two pars I would be hard to beat. I didn't. Instead I hit it into the water on the long par-three seventeenth, made double bogey, and finished tied for third—one shot out of the playoff between Lou and John. Lou went on to win.

The following year I finished second to Raymond Floyd at the Masters, but he won by eight shots. He was superb, shooting 65 in the final round, but I felt I won my own little tournament. I was getting my feet wet. I was getting closer, playing good golf, getting up there in contention, and seeing how I had to eliminate mistakes to win a major. That was the year I won three times and finished second to Jack on the money list.

In 1977, I led going into the final round of the Masters and was three shots back at the British Open, but took big tumbles. I played loose golf at the Masters and finished tied for eighth behind winner Tom Watson. Then, at Turnberry, I shot a third-round 66 to pull within three of Watson and Nicklaus with eighteen left to play. The final round? That belonged to the titanic battle between Jack and Tom. I stumbled, tied for fifth, and had to lick my wounds again, but it started a string of five consecutive top eight finishes in the British for me.

The following year at St. Andrews, I put myself in position again. I was tied for the second-round lead with Seve and Isao Aoki, but a third-round 73 left me trailing Watson and Peter Oosterhuis by one. Jack shot a closing 69 to win his third British Open while I closed with a 71 and tied for second—two shots back—with Tom Kite, Raymond, and Simon Owen.

I had played well in 1979 and was tied for the lead at Royal Lytham until I double-bogeyed the seventy-first hole. I knew teeing off that if I could keep the ball in the fairway, make a par, and do something on the eighteenth, I might tie Seve. But my drive landed three feet into the rough, then I smothered a 2-iron into a bunker. That really hurt, but I have to admit that Seve played incredible golf. He had some fantastic escapes, including that birdie at sixteen from the car park. I tied Jack for second.

The following month at Oakland Hills, I really thought I had won my first major. At the time I was one of only two players to shoot four subpar rounds in a PGA Championship—Arnold was the other—and not win. Honestly, I didn't have any business even making a playoff, but David Graham doubled the last hole to tie me. Then I didn't have any business losing the playoff, but I did.

On the first hole I lagged my approach putt to two feet for par and David, after two loose shots, had only one chance—to knock in an improbable twenty-five-footer for par. And he did. Then on the second, I hit the best 4-wood of my life and had it twelve feet for eagle, which burned the lip. David matched my tap-in birdie with a ten-footer of his own. On the third hole I hit into a bunker and virtually handed it to David, who hit it ten feet from the hole.

After that there was a lot of bridesmaid-but-never-a-bride talk about me. A lot of it really was justified.

I added another second place at the 1983 Masters when Tom Kite and I tied, four shots behind Seve. Seve started birdie-eagle-par-birdie that final day and just played magically. What he did was awesome.

Gentle Ben? The crowds were still behind me, and I was searching for a lot of things—peace in my personal life, consistency, and a way to win that first major. Little did I know that a year later, I'd be standing alongside Seve at the green jacket ceremony.

7.

AUGUSTA

FAVORITE U.S. COURSES

Augusta National (the way it used to be)
Chicago Golf Club
Pine Valley
National Golf Links
Winged Foot
Sand Hills
Cypress Point

It was a bright, crisp morning—the kind that makes you realize spring really is just around the corner. I was standing on the lawn underneath that stately old oak tree that spreads its limbs across the back of the clubhouse, shooting several promos for CBS' upcoming telecast of the 1996 Masters. As I stood there, the memories and emotions washed over me, touching my heart as they had so often over these past eleven months.

Julie and my two oldest girls were in the clubhouse. Arthur Williams, the club's maitre d', had taken Katherine, then eight and a half, up to the Crow's Nest to show her where I stayed when I played there as an amateur. Claire, just four, was exploring every nook and cranny she could find. Before we started shooting, I had shown Katherine around the ground floor, pointing out the trophy, which sits on a table in the lobby most of the year, pictures of Bobby Jones, and faded photographs of the club as it was in its earliest days.

We had lunch later in the Trophy Room, where no introductions were necessary. The staff knew the girls from our Christmas cards and welcomed them, as they always did with Julie and me, as family. "I want you to know how special your daddy is here," one waiter said, launching into yet another story.

A few hours later we were on our way to Orlando and I was searching my heart for just the right words to explain to Katherine just why this place called Augusta National is so special to me.

"Katherine, I think you got a sense of how people feel about you over there," I said. "When you're older, you'll perhaps come back one day and understand how much this course and tournament have meant to me. Isn't the place gorgeous? Isn't it different? Aren't the people special?"

I told her about more of the people and spoke of the majesty of Magnolia Lane. I explained that it was where I had won two majors—two green jackets; that it was a part of me.

Suddenly, I was crying.

Katherine hugged me. She was already used to those heart-on-the-sleeve emotions of mine, but I think she saw something even deeper that day. She saw the passion I feel every time I step onto that course.

I could give you a million reasons why I love Augusta; why it's as exciting as your first date, as exhilarating as a ride on a giant wooden roller coaster, and as comfortable as an old shoe.

There's simply nothing else like it.

The first time I walked onto the course I saw it had a majesty and a grandeur I had never felt on a golf course. I was struck by the spaciousness of the course, the scale, and the hills. And the touch of formality that was Jones.

The whole place is a reflection of him. You get the feeling that if they added anything, it would be out of place. I think they purposely left things out when they built it. And the clubhouse. The architecture is so simple, down to the screen doors and the block letters on the brass plaques. It was purposely underdone to highlight the course.

And Magnolia Lane? It's art—a beautiful canopy that leads you down the lane to a little light in the clubhouse hall.

Charles Price describes Jones as a reflection of the lessons and values he learned in life. One bit of his philosophy was perfection in character; the other was something an oriental philosopher once wrote: "The single flower has more inherent beauty than the bouquet." When I think of Augusta, I think of that because everything's stripped away. That's the simplicity.

Price emphasized what was left out when Jones and Dr. Alister MacKenzie built the course rather than what was put in. That guided Jones' thinking, and I've always been fascinated by that—and Jones himself.

In fact, a whole area of my study is a tribute to Jones. I've read his writings. I've studied his life, his career, and his character and understood at young age how much he meant to American golf. And, now, to me.

It's ironic that Augusta and Jones are such a part of me, yet I never had the chance to meet him. I was excited about the prospect when I qualified for my first Masters in 1972, but Jones died just before Christmas in 1971. I certainly had plans to go shake his hand and would have loved to have met him, even though he was ill, because the course is so much of his being. So much of what he was able to do and achieve in golf are what Augusta National is and what it stands for.

And so much of what I am was influenced by him.

"You keep reading what Bobby Jones had to write about," Harvey always said. "It makes sense."

Jones wrote in beautiful, fluent language that painted vivid pictures in my mind. They're still the best words about golf from any player that I've ever read. And his career? Here is a man who won the hearts of the world and the Grand Slam in 1930 and remained the most humble champion golf has ever seen. As rare, in fact, as his Grand Slam.

As O. B. Keeler said of Jones' four majors in 1930, "Others may attack—in vain—forever."

Like everyone else, he suffered early in his career. And he had a hot, hot, hot temper. Yes, he was very much a competitor, but he also battled himself unbelievably. He was expected to win everything by the time he was fifteen, and he had a very tough time winning his first one. But when he did, the floodgates opened. And when he was on top of the world, he was a model of restraint. That drew people to him.

Golf aside, he was the consummate gentleman. An extremely well educated man—he had degrees from Georgia Tech and Harvard, and passed the bar after just two years of law school—Jones displayed courtly manners and exuded good taste wherever he went. He never overdid anything. Golf was a game, yet something very dear to him. He played so few rounds of golf, it's astounding to discover he won major championships as an amateur. He dusted off his clubs when the spring came around each year and put them up in September, and most of the time he was playing he was also attending law school at Emory University in Atlanta.

His manner was so gracious. His acceptance speeches were always extremely modest and quite brief, and his letter writing was brilliant. He would get to the point in a letter in just the right way with a terrific touch and knowledge of the English language and, like his golf course, his letters were perfect. They still study them for form and content at the law school at Emory. And, despite his great knowledge, which allowed him to talk about most anything, he had a way of making everyone feel very comfortable around him.

His writings are intellectual, but he still managed to put it all in human terms. He always gave advice that beginning players or average players could really sink their teeth into as well as good suggestions for the expert player. And that's hard to do.

He revealed so much of himself over the years. It was not above him to admit that he felt entirely nervous and even nauseous at a tournament. He would let people in to truly know him, telling them of the fears of playing in a tournament or championship. He let his guard down and made everything so human—a trait I consider genius.

One of Jones' most famous lines about the game—he came up with it when he was twenty-five—was his description of a golfer as "the dogged victim of inexorable fate." Dan Jenkins wound up borrowing that line as a title for one of his collections of golf stories. Jones' descriptive phrases always had a very poetic or artistic way about them. He said things, at twenty-five, such as, "Golf is a game that burns inwardly and sears the soul." Perspectives like that are so rare. Especially at such a young age.

Clifford Roberts, his partner in developing Augusta National, was very different from Jones, but it's that rare combination that made Augusta—and the Masters—what it is today. Roberts was a very meticulous man and his attention to detail will always be part of the fabric of the course and the tournament. Augusta National really was his mistress and he admitted it. He was totally devoted to that place. He envisioned the lasting success that would come from his collaboration with Jones.

Carl Jackson, my caddie at Augusta National since 1976, once told me a story that puts Roberts' hold on the club into perspective. Carl kept noticing this big great horned owl that sat up in a pine tree to the left of the sixth tee box and pointed it out to me. We kept our eyes on it, watching it, studying it. The caddies even nicknamed him Mr. Roberts and that owl sort of became part of the golf course. But the day Clifford Roberts took his life, those caddies swear that owl left that pine tree and never came back.

I did have the chance to meet Roberts, which was kind of like meeting Ben Hogan. He was the autocrat. Everybody knew he ran the place, and you knew you had to be on your best behavior when you were with him. I met him at my first Masters, right outside the main part of the clubhouse, and he couldn't have been nicer. Or more to the point:

"Mr. Roberts, I am Ben Crenshaw," I said, extending my hand.

He said he hoped I would play well, noting that they were quite fond of Texans at Augusta. Then he paused and looked at me. "By the way," he said, "you know we have a barber shop on the grounds."

He wasn't kidding. I went right in there and got a haircut.

The way he did it, it wasn't something that you got mad about. He looked at you square in the eyes just like that wise old owl. Maybe there really was something to that old owl in the pine tree after all.

Roberts was the man who set the rule that you couldn't hit an extra ball during practice rounds, and signs reading—"Practice rounds. Use one ball only"—remain at the first, tenth, and all par-three tees. He's also the only man who, when they added those bunkers to the left at eighteen, deemed it one bunker. And that's the way it was—even though there were two.

He was meticulous even to the end. He systematically knew how he was going to end his own life and even asked his assistant, Bettie Yonker, to buy him new pajamas. It was almost mystical. He was ill and had been on a trip, and when he got back he was very weak. His regular club waiter, Ray Wigfall, helped him walk to the first tee and he asked if the huge house behind the first green was still standing. He had wanted it torn down and when Wigfall assured him it was gone, he was satisfied.

Later that night, he asked an Augusta security guard to help him load his gun. He was found near Eisenhower's Pond, dead of a self-inflicted gunshot wound.

Roberts' suicide had a profound effect upon the club and staff, but Augusta is still about the people. The club is part of their being and they make you feel as though you're part of their family. Bill Lane, a former tournament chairman and Houstonian who died in the late '70s, offered me a ride back to Texas in his private plane after the 1976

Masters. He was on the official pin setters and tee markers committee at the time and didn't really know me. He was such a nice man.

And the staff. Arthur Williams. Frank Carpenter, the wine steward. The men in the locker room over the years—Council Dandridge, C. Y. Yount, Roland Gray, Hugene Hughes. Front office manager Bettie Yonker and executive tournament secretaries Wilda Gwin and Kathryn Murphy. Caddie master Freddie Bennett and nursery superintendent Tommy—no relation—Crenshaw. Those guards in the gatehouse that you haven't seen in so long. It's just such a warm feeling there.

My career is so closely tied with Augusta National and the Masters that maybe I have a deeper feeling for it. Maybe I am blinded by the fact that I've won there twice. My deepest feelings lie with that place, but there are a million other reasons why Hale Irwin, Curtis Strange, and others who won more than one U.S. Open can tell you how special it is to win the national championship, too.

I know you must think I'm a bit over the top about Augusta National, but there's no place that stirs my emotions like that golf course. It can be utterly exhilarating and it can be utterly disappointing—on the same hole. You can hit it in the water on a course where you're given all the space in the world. Players don't see problems like that in other major championships.

Jackie Burke put it best when he said, "It's the most tempting golf course in the world." The conditions and the problems there put you in that position where you are tempted. You can play it safe or you can really chance it and pull off a shot that is truly rewarding.

Everyone knows the story of Augusta National—how it used to be a nursery, and how Jones and Roberts chose it as the site for an exclusive golf club where their friends would be able to play. And what Jones and architect Dr. MacKenzie built and completed in 1932 was a dramatic piece of landscaping never seen before in this country—a course totally devoid of rough and entirely accessible for anybody to play within his handicap.

Even more fascinating to me are all the efforts of so many to make it flourish. The club struggled during the Depression and nearly went broke three times. But it survived. So did the tournament, which began in 1934 and received legendary status the following year when Gene Sarazen made his famous double eagle on number fifteen.

What made Augusta National so unusual was the risk-reward design, the formality, and the thought of holding a formal tournament in the South. I'm always tickled to hear people talk about seeing it for the first time.

It's overwhelming and absolutely bigger than you think. Television really doesn't do it justice. It's so hilly and has some of the most beautiful trees and plants and landscapes peacefully coexisting with the property. Your eyes just wander across that landscape; there are no limits to what you can see.

Rae's Creek meanders through the property, and all the azaleas, dogwoods, and other plants reflect the nursery that they were born in and how they were nurtured. The combination is truly magnificent—and stunning the first time you take it all in. So many places have tried to emulate it, but they will never be able to recreate it.

I'm sure I've seen many things there that others may not have seen, but someone is always pointing out something new. One day while playing a round with Steve Elkington, who's a big gardener, we were on the second hole when he pointed out orange azaleas to the left. They were orange—like tangerines. Nothing I'd ever seen before. Augusta National is filled with things like that. We're all still learning and discovering together there.

I always get asked about my favorite holes at Augusta National and I have to say I'm enthralled by the fifth and fourteenth greens. They are two of the damnedest greens I have ever seen in my life and are designed to portray St. Andrews. Both Jones and MacKenzie wanted to have at least a touch of St. Andrews on their course and found it in the roll of the upward slopes of these greens. Those front

Mom always had a smile on her face . . . at least
when Charlie and I weren't causing trouble.
(Bonnie Boorman)

Bonnie and Charlie look on as I
try on my new catcher's mitt.
(Pearl Crenshaw)

I was a pitcher, a catcher, and a pretty decent
hitter—until I decided to focus on golf.
(Charles Crenshaw)

I wish my finish still looked like it
did when I was nine.
(Charles Crenshaw)

(The Crenshaw Family Archives)

My game was starting to take shape during my high school years.
(Jerry Click)

At the Texas Junior with Tom Kite and Bob Elliott (1967).
(Scott Sayers collection)

Signing with the University of Texas was one of my best moves ever. *(left to right)* Coach George Hannon, me, Dad, Coach Darrell Royal. *(Courtesy of Bob Rochs, University of Texas)*

The 1971 UT golf team. We won national championships in 1971 and 1972. *(Courtesy of Bill Little, University of Texas)*

I went crazy after making a twenty-foot putt to tie Tom for medalist in the 1972 NCAA Championship.
(Kerry Merritt)

Sand on my face and a pound of hair on my head, at the NCAAs in Cape Coral, Florida, 1972.
(Lane Stewart, "Sports Illustrated")

In 1972 there was no provision for a playoff, so Tom and I
shared the NCAA low individual trophy. *(Kerry Merritt)*

(George Hannon)

"Little Ben" and I have been through a lot together. *(Jerry Click)*

(Brian deGraffenreid)

With my friend Carl Jackson at the Masters.
(Frank Christian)

When Tom and I filmed "The Little Red Video" and "The Little Green Video" for Mickey Holden, these were the only times Harvey let Tom and me hit balls together. *(Courtesy of Mickey Holden and Bob Daemmrich)*

On the set with Tom, Harvey, and Mickey Holden. *(Karlene Gilbeau)*

When you hole a bunker shot like I did on Friday in the 1984 Masters,
you begin to think it might be your week.
(John Iacono, "Sports Illustrated")

On the tenth green at Augusta in 1984. Making this putt on Sunday was perhaps the biggest putt of my life... I would've laid down and died for a two-putt! *(Phil Sheldon)*

My dad and stepmother Bobbie, following the "Green Jacket" ceremony in 1984.
(*Frank Christian, Augusta National*)

My friend, agent, and business manager Scotty Sayers at the Augusta Par 3 tournament. My dad warned me to never win it like I did in 1987. He was afraid of the "jinx." I bogeyed the seventy-first hole in the Masters that year to miss the playoff by one stroke.
(*Howdy Giles*)

The Texans: With Byron Nelson, possibly golf's greatest gentleman. *(Roger Cleveland)*

I always enjoy spending time with former President Bush, who is a great supporter of golf. *(Julie Crenshaw)*

Mr. Hogan with my daughter Katherine. He had a soft side that most people never saw. *(The Crenshaw Family Archives)*

In Scotland with Glen Campbell, Jack Nicklaus, and Sean Connery.
(The Crenshaw Family Archives)

With Gerald Ford. When I played with President Ford in the Memphis Open, he made a hole in one on the seventh hole. *(Dave Darnell)*

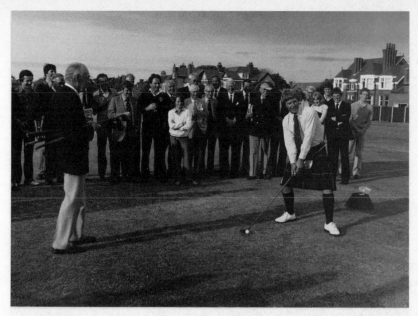

Herb Wind will always be the "dean" of American golf writers. *(Brian Morgan)*

Bobbie Millen, who caddies for me overseas and has been a friend for twenty-five years, enjoys golf history as much as I do. Here we pay our respects to young Tom Morris. *(M. Nouillan; Thomson & Co.)*

I love playing The Old Course. It is THE best place in the world to study golf course architecture, which is one of my passions. *(John Cuban, Allsport)*

The eighth hole at the Sand Hills. When Bill and I saw this property, we couldn't believe our good fortune. *(Jim Kidd)*

I feel very fortunate to have Bill Coore as my partner in the golf course design business. We try to keep it simple. *(Dick Durrance)*

Our Coore & Crenshaw associates, whom we affectionately call "The Boys," are true artists. They bring our visions to life. *(Pat Bridges)*

Winning the World Cup in 1988 with Mark McCumber was especially meaningful at one of my favorite golf courses, Royal Melbourne. *(Julie Crenshaw)*

Before this, I had never given a putting lesson on a pool table, let alone to one of world's greatest putters, Phil Mickelson. *(Julie Crenshaw)*

faces are dangerous and you don't see anything else like them in this country.

And, nothing else is prettier than Amen Corner. The whole place is magnificent, it really is. Many words have been written about Augusta, but it is still indescribable and untouchable. You just can't grasp it, but it's out there. There is nothing as stirring to your soul as being on that part of the course.

Back there is where the tournament unfolds on Sunday. The acoustics are such that the sounds rumble right across those pine trees until they almost seem to vibrate. If not for that beautiful expanse of land and those big trees, the sounds wouldn't carry like they do. But nothing else is anywhere close to it in golf. Players know where the sound is coming from, who is playing, and what that player made on the hole. I mean it. You know what an eagle roar sounds like and you know what a par and a birdie sound like. And the decibel level when Jack Nicklaus makes an eagle just shakes the trees. It is truly amazing. But I guess it's only fitting. What else would you expect from the most amazing golf course on earth?

I could talk forever about Augusta and Roberts and Jones. I could tell you a million more wonderful things about it—like rummaging through a lost-club barrel there and finding one of Betsy Cullen's putters, one that Mickey Wright had given her—but I'll refrain.

However, I will leave you with my favorite story about Jones and what he meant to the game, to Augusta, and to me.

I've always said that the size of Jones' cabin says as much about him as anything. It is the smallest cabin on the property, but it sat on the nicest spot—like a little toy box.

Charlie Price befriended Jones late in life, and when it got to the point where Jones could never go out—he had a disease as rare as he is called syringomelia, which attacks the spinal cord—he would have runners bring him information and scores to that cabin. Charlie was one of his runners and one day they sat, had a scotch, and were thinking about things. Charlie looked at a man he admired so much and was thinking what life had meant to this man who had been a pinnacle of sports and the illness he was going through. And Charlie Price—like I am now—allowed a tear to drop down his cheek.

"Charlie, we won't have any of that," Jones said. "We all must play the ball as it lies."

There was simply no one like him; no place like the one he created.

8.

FINALLY

WHAT MAKES
AUGUSTA SPECIAL

Magnolia Lane
Amen Corner
Southern hospitality
Pairing sheets
Scoreboards
Spaciousness
Azaleas
Pimento cheese sandwiches
The patrons
Sounds and cheers
The "crow's nest"

John Griffith and Bobby Kay were going crazy. They were darting around the clubhouse, peeking into the locker room, eyeing the range, keeping watch near the parking lot. They were looking everywhere and couldn't find me. They just knew I had overslept.

Here it was Sunday morning of the '84 Masters and I still had four holes to play to finish the third round. A rainstorm had dumped rain and hail on the course Saturday afternoon and play was called at 5:30. I was playing with Tom Watson, who had marked a fifteen-foot birdie try at the thirteenth. I had an eighty-foot eagle attempt that looked as though it ran from here to Macon, but I cozied it up there to two feet for birdie and went to sleep two shots off that delayed third-round lead.

No one could find me. At least not until they came out to the four-teenth hole where I was—in their words—communing with nature.

That would be the start to one of the longest, most exciting days of my then-thirty-two-year-old life. It would be the day I erased all the doubts from my mind and everyone else's; a day that would begin with a frantic search by two close friends and end with Steve and Larry Gatlin—decked out in their jammies—standing on their heads in the entry hall to the house I'd rented just around the corner from the club. A day where everything came together so perfectly; the day I won my first green jacket—for myself and my friends.

Just where those four days came from, I'm not sure. I was tired of losing majors, that's certain. Nearly a dozen chances to win majors—and no titles—were beginning to put worries in my head, and Augusta was no place for that. But I was beginning to feel my way around this course really well and, for once, I came in relaxed and with one thing on my mind—winning.

Two big reasons—my first wife Polly and I had agreed to an ami-cable divorce, ending a difficult and tumultuous few years in my life and allowing me to take a deep breath, and I was playing well. I'd just closed with a 67 in Greensboro to finish tied for third and came in ready to play. And I had made a few changes to my game, includ-ing weakening my left hand a bit in my grip. These were about to pay off.

During the practice rounds I got a reminder from Jackie Burke, a mentor to me as always. Jackie, who won the 1956 Masters and PGA, told me a story about the famous Russian pianist Vladimir Horowitz, who, no matter how large the concert hall, kept his focus on the piano keys. That hit home. I blocked out everything else and concentrated on fairways and greens.

As I look back, things were coming together. I had peace of mind about my personal life, my game was clicking, and my close friends and Dad were there to keep me loose. I was rooming with the Gatlins that week, although Larry took off for the Caymans with his wife, leaving the Gatlin Brothers' big ol' tour bus parked outside the house.

I'm always ready for that first round at Augusta. No more practice rounds, interview sessions, and so forth, which are all nice and necessary, but none of them are the main event. Lucky for me, I started out of the gate like I was double-parked outside. I shot a 67—my lowest opening round at Augusta—and took the lead by one shot over Lee Trevino and two shots over Isao Aoki, David Graham, Mark Lye, and Tom Purtzer. It was a lot better than the 76 I'd opened with the previous year.

This time around I was so accurate it was uncanny. I hit all but two fairways and all but one green and did not make a bogey. Other than that it was sort of routine. Yes, I'm kidding. I had made a couple of changes in my bag, pulling the 1-iron out and sticking a 4-wood in there. And I was using an old driver, one I found in a barrel at a pro shop in Houston and paid three hundred dollars for. I just liked its feel and, although I was probably hitting the ball a little shorter with it, it suited me. So did my new irons from Walter Hagen.

Friday I held it together. Five birdies, five bogeys. I also holed a really impossible bunker shot at number nine, the first of three birdies in a row. I'd missed some birdies on the back side and made bogey at eighteen when I missed a four-footer, but that bunker shot at the ninth kept sticking in my mind and I wasn't worried. It really started me believing. I just had this sort of feeling, started seeing some things and doing some things out of the ordinary and I thought, this could be a week where I really contend. And I hung in there. I was tied for third with Graham and Nick Faldo.

When play was called Saturday, Mark was still ahead at nine-under but he was only through eleven holes. I was at seven-under after I made the decision to go ahead and finish the thirteenth hole. When I lined up that eighty-foot eagle, I felt good about getting the ball to stop somewhere down around the hole and coaxing a two-putt birdie out of the thing. I had a nice feeling for my putts that day, and an eagle or birdie would be a nice way to end a rain-shortened day.

There were still nineteen of us on the course when play resumed at 8 A.M. Sunday and, even though it would be a long day, we all knew that with so much at stake, what the heck? We'd finish the third round, leave, and not tee off for the final round until two or later.

That late time has worn on players for years. You love to play late on Saturday and Sunday, but at 2:30 at Augusta? I'm an early riser and there are just so many papers you can read. It is excruciating, especially at a major championship, where you are so keyed up and you want to get out there and play, but you're waiting around. And waiting is hard for me. You go to sleep real well the night before, but you get up and the next morning you start thinking about your round and planning your round, and it is agonizing. You have too much time.

Even after 1984, I went off late in 1987, 1988, and 1989, because in all three of those Masters, I was right there. And that wait? Good night! It's just awful. When we were younger we got into the habit of playing basketball on the driveway to pass the time. Now we've taken to chipping pine cones in the front yard. Our bodies aren't what they used to be.

That morning I finished up the third round with five straight fours and went right to the airport to pick up Larry. He had flown all night—on a 3 A.M. flight from New York to Atlanta—but he was ready to go. I went back to the house to take a nap and he and Steve went to breakfast.

I felt as though I'd missed a couple of putts I should have had, including a twelve-footer for birdie at the eighteenth. I did manage to sleep for about an hour and a half before I went back out, which is very rare for me.

I felt refreshed starting that final round and went out in 33, the same as Larry Nelson, and I birdied the eighth and the ninth, where I made a real nice right-to-left-breaking twelve-footer. Then came the magic at the tenth.

I hit a so-so drive and I had a 3-iron left. I just wanted to get it up on the green and make a four and get out of there, but I was sixty feet from the hole and the pin was back left. I remember that I was hoping for a two-putt, and I heard those handheld blowers they use to blow off those little burrs from the trees. A few were left out on the green and I was a little concerned because when a surface is so smooth, like this, any little imperfection is going to show up. But there was Carl, holding that pin.

We had agreed on a line and I stroked this putt. I tried to keep the putt high because I had about an eight- or nine-foot break to the left. I wanted to give it a chance to just kind of fall into the hole or, more realistically, get it within a six-foot circle. I thought maybe I hit it a little too hard, but it slowed down just a little bit, about three-quarters of the way to the hole. Then, that ball just found the bottom of the cup.

"Oh my Lord!" I said. "Good night, this is one that I really didn't expect." A two-putt four would have been golden at that point. But then it went in.

I kept telling myself I had to calm down. That birdie was really something unexpected—an unbelievable putt at that time—and it gave me a two-shot lead over Kite.

I immediately made bogey at number eleven when I hit my approach shot to the right and didn't get it up and down, but you know what? I didn't let that bother me too much because of that stroke on the tenth. I really stole one or two there.

Then I birdied the twelfth, hitting a 6-iron to about twelve feet from the pin, which was back right. Now, no one goes for the pin at number twelve, but that's what it looked like. That is the most elusive, nerve-racking hole because you're never sure of your club. It's very much a feel hole and you hit it, then hope and pray a gust of wind doesn't come up. Great shots there have turned into disasters because of the wind. It's wrecked a lot of hopes.

This time it helped win the tournament for me. Both Nelson and

Kite, who was playing behind me, hit into the water—Nelson for a double bogey; Kite for a triple. Afterward, John Griffith couldn't believe I'd gone for the pin, and I hadn't. I pushed the shot and it came up okay.

"Well," John said, more than a bit relieved, "I thought you were smarter than that."

I've made my share of doubles there and they sting. They hurt like the dickens. But this birdie put the tournament in my hands. It was all up to me . . . and whatever the forces of Augusta held for me.

That twelfth hole, the middle hole of Amen Corner, is at the very bottommost part of the course. The wind swirls in and swirls out, making it the most intimidating hole I have ever seen. It forces you to hit an exacting shot which you can't feel right about unless it's dead calm. And it never is.

Hit it anywhere short and you expect it to go into the water, but pray it lands in a bunker. Long is just as bad. It's a seemingly innocent chip—you've seen thousands of chip shots played from back there—but it is the hardest thing in the world to get that ball going at the right pace because you have to play a shot through the fringe. And don't loft the ball, because if you do or if you catch it a little thin it could easily go across the green into the water.

It is simply one of the great little pieces of architecture in the world. It's very dramatic. The gallery is right there with you at the tee, and then you sort of descend in silence across Hogan's Bridge. It's true that the only sounds you can hear back there are your heartbeat and your caddie's heartbeat. You're just trying to get out of there. It's like taking hold of a snake, I suppose. You just hold your breath.

When that putt fell in for a three-shot lead, I knew I could breathe again.

At the thirteenth I hit my tee shot onto the fairway and debated whether I should go for the green, but I kind of looked back over my shoulder and saw that Tom had hit it in the water. I wanted to knock the ball up onto the green with my 4-wood, but I looked over in the crowd and thought I saw Billy Joe Patton. Patton, who was serving as a rules committeeman at Augusta, had lost the chance in 1954 to become the only amateur to win the Masters when he went for both the thirteenth and fifteenth greens in two and landed in the water both places.

Because of that, I laid up, scrambled for par, and, well, you know the rest. Patton, it turns out, wasn't in the crowd that day, but it didn't matter. Just the image saved me from making one of those regrettable mistakes.

On the way in I pulled my drive at fourteen, overdrew my approach, and wound up with a twenty-footer for par. I had to putt across this innocuous, small hump on the right side of the green that's like a magnet, affecting everything. The ball got up the slope, started down fast and . . . went in. That desperate putt meant more than the one at number ten because it held things together. And the twelve-foot birdie I made at the fifteenth? That calmed me down on the way home.

At eighteen I drove the middle of the fairway, hit a 5-iron to the center of the green, and two-putted. It was over. I had won the Masters, eleven years after finishing as the low amateur for the second year in a row, and with my father beaming as Seve Ballesteros slipped the green jacket onto my shoulders. It was such a special moment for Dad. And not because he grew up in Alabama, but because he loved Augusta so much.

When that final putt fell in, the one thing I felt was relief. I went through it like everybody else who wins their first one, and it was tortuous. It's torture doubting yourself. You always feel capable of winning, but it's one hell of a thing to prove it to yourself.

When I went back to the house that night I opened the door and there were Larry and Steve standing on their heads—an inverted salute, of sorts. I knew just how they felt. I felt like I was standing on my head, too.

We stayed up channel surfing, drinking, watching the highlights on television and playing gin rummy. We fell asleep about 1:30 and I was completely exhausted.

The next day Harvey was standing there when I stepped off the plane. He flopped his hand out for me to hold and looked at me with those loving eyes.

"Mighty proud of you," he said.

9.

LONE STAR LEGACY

BEST TEXAS PLAYERS

Ben Hogan	Babe Zaharias
Byron Nelson	Lee Trevino
Jimmy Demaret	Lloyd Mangrum
Tom Kite	Judy Rankin
Jackie Burke	Don January
Ralph Guldahl	Miller Barber

. . . and on, and on, and on

Willie Nelson was just standing there, leaning on a limestone pillar at Bull Creek Inn, waiting to go onstage one last time. He'd just come back from Nashville and the country—not just Texas—was beginning to understand how special his music is.

I must have been a sophomore or junior at Texas and couldn't resist the chance to introduce myself. He was good friends with Coach Royal, he loved golf, and he lived in Austin. We had three things in common right there. It was late—around midnight—and we had a nice little conversation. I don't know what possessed me, but suddenly I asked him, "What time is it?"

Willie looked down at his watch and said, "I don't know. It ain't got no little hand."

That threw me for a loop, but I couldn't stop. "Where you gonna play next?"

He paused. "Shreveport. But they haven't come to get me yet."

Willie. He's one of a kind. A man with a battered guitar and his own golf course where par is whatever you want to make it on a given day. He loves the game and plays every chance he gets. He's even been known to use his Mercedes as a cart during the winter, driving it down his fairways and playing out of his trunk.

One day he was playing with Coach Royal in the Legends of Golf pro-am at Onion Creek and he got stuck behind two trees. Coach asked him what he was going to do.

"I think I'll just shoot up amongst here and if I hit something," he said, "I'll just say I'm unlucky."

Stories. Legends. Characters. Texas golf history is filled with them. And, yes, we're as proud of that rich legacy—the richest this side of the Atlantic, I have to say—as we are of being the only state that was once its own nation.

Whether it's playing eighteen with Willie and Coach Royal, who knows just about everyone in the world; hitting balls while Hogan kept a watchful eye; listening to Dave Marr's stories; soaking in one of Harvey's lessons; or laughing so hard at one of Lee Trevino's jokes that I thought I'd never get off the first tee, it's all a part of what made me what I am today. And, quite simply, it's a big part of growing up in Texas; part of a legacy.

Texans joke that we didn't invent golf, but just about perfected it. I laugh, but those folks may not really be that far off.

Hogan pretty much invented practice, and Byron Nelson owns the one record in the game that may never be broken—nineteen wins in one year. Marr was one of the smoothest players ever to touch a club; Trevino was one of the funniest. Jimmy Demaret reminded us long into every song-filled night that golf is a game, then, later in life, he went out and threw a lawn party for the legends of the game that gave rise to the Senior Tour.

And Jackie Burke? He may be the most irascible philosopher, teacher, and mentor the game has ever seen.

It's not that I didn't grow up idolizing Jack Nicklaus and Arnold Palmer, because I did. Arnold will always be The King. When he speaks, people listen, and he is so kind. He gives so much to people it is unbelievable. I've never seen anybody like him. And Jack? He's simply the best ever to play the game.

He was way up there in my mind and I was nervous as hell when I met him. We were in the locker room at Merion one day and there weren't many people around so I thought it would be a good time to introduce myself. I decided to take a chance. He was in the bathroom and I thought, "I've got him now, I'll corner him."

There were two urinals in there and I stuck my hand out.

"Jack, I'm Ben Crenshaw from Austin."

He looked at me a bit strangely. "Oh, I will be right with you."

How embarrassing was that? That's how in awe I was. When I reminded him of the story later, he just laughed so hard. I guess it was quite a first impression.

Jack leaves a lot of people tongue-tied—and in awe. The most amazing thing about him isn't just the eighteen majors he won, but the fact that he contended in almost every major he played for so long. He finished either second or third twenty-three times in the four majors combined, which is absolutely astounding. If you figure he might have won a third of those times, that would be twenty-six major championships. Or twenty-eight if you count those two Amateurs. And Jack does.

That says something about his powers of concentration, which are stronger than just about anybody's. He and Hogan. And Tiger. They all have the ability to block out everything.

But even with Jack and Arnold creating legends right in front of my eyes, the great Texas players had a profound effect on my career.

Texas is so rich in great players and stories that the history was just ingrained in us over the years and inspired the younger generations.

And believe me, we had a lot to live up to. We knew about Nelson's records, Hogan's Grand Slam, and Demaret's three Masters, but that wasn't all. Through all those stories everyone told, we knew about Hogan's cold precision; about Demaret's cashmere sweaters and night-club tunes, Nelson's huge hands the size of a catcher's mitt, Titanic Thompson's adventures in hustling, and Trevino's secret club—a sixteen-ounce Dr Pepper bottle wrapped in adhesive tape.

We just knew everything about them. And, if you were one of the up-and-coming players—even as a junior—they knew about you. For a big state it is really a pretty small place when it comes to golf.

I had Nelson and Hogan at the top of my list. What they did was so incredible. I thought they were almost infallible. I watched Hogan hit balls and I've never seen a ball hit like that. Just faultless, to the point where you didn't think you were worthy at all.

One day when I was struggling with my game I asked Dave Marr if he'd ever seen Hogan hit a bad shot or show his temper. Dave said it was rare, but yes. "The bad shots he hit, he quickly rectified," Dave said. "But I've seen him tear up the lips of a few bunkers."

You have no idea what that meant to me. It took a little pressure off of me. I had visions of these players so conjured in my mind, it was like I could never live up to them. Dave reminded me that they, too, were human.

Dave and I spent a lot of time together over the years and I learned so much. We became closer through our mutual friend, Mickey van Gerbig. Dave was close to both Hogan and Nelson and he learned to play, compete, and fight with them; he also learned to laugh with them. They had made a huge difference in his life. In turn, he made a huge difference in mine.

As my first Ryder Cup captain he was fabulous. He set a very high standard for all of us to follow and was smooth, very suave. Dave had spent all that time in New York—Dan Jenkins called him the pro from 52nd Street—but he was pure Texas. He'd grown up in Houston, play-ing Memorial Park and learning from Demaret and Burke and even

Tommy Bolt. He was so funny with his great sense of humor and great expressions, and that made him a truly gracious announcer when he went to television.

Dave would never say anything bad about someone. He wasn't going to tear anyone down. And he elevated the game, tried to make the game better.

A few years before both he and Hogan died, Dave was in Fort Worth and called Hogan. "Ben, we need to go to lunch. We haven't talked in a long while."

They had more fun talking about the good old days and the characters they had met. "I really want to thank you for doing that," Hogan said, cleaning his glasses. "God, I miss tournament golf."

Every time Dave told that story, my heart went out to Mr. Hogan.

People always talk about how cold Hogan was, but I disagree. He just would not put up with any nonsense. One thing he positively could not abide was a total stranger coming up and asking him something about golf. Hogan couldn't handle that and he made no pretense that he could. But with people he knew, he was warm. I remember him playing with Katherine when she was just a baby. And he and I had some nice, long talks.

Hogan was an impeccable dresser. Whatever he wore was always of the finest quality, and also extremely conservative. The crease in his pants? You could cut your finger on it. He just looked like a professional and had an air, a presence, about him. You could tell from the way this man dressed that he took pride in his work and put playing golf on a pedestal.

You could feel that presence when you were with him. He was very emphatic, very confident, and when he chose to drive home a point, it would make the hairs on your neck stand up. You believed it.

We usually talked about golf equipment, and he was unusually precise in his views. And, he was extremely particular about his clubs. I had a MacGregor driver that I loved—a Tommy Armour model—and he asked to see it. He inspected it, turned it upside down, looked at the face. That was the first time I'd ever seen someone look at a club upside down.

Finally he said, "Looks like a goddamn doorknob."

That just totally deflated me.

He told me to go pick up one of his clubs. "Mr. Hogan," I said, "the face of this club is absolutely dead flat. It has got no radius or bulge on it."

He kind of looked at me real strange and said, "An iron doesn't have any radius or bulge on it, does it?"

That just hit me between the eyes. This is a wood we're talking about—a persimmon wood. I still have one at home that's the flattest, most unhittable club—it has no loft. Hogan could hit it because it was bored flat to get him to compensate for his hook, but he gave one to Jackie Burke and Jackie said he hit nothing but duck slices.

Hogan was one of a kind. He had to overcome so much in his career—not just that hook. Like so many players from that era, he grew up in a caddie yard, only he shared his with Nelson at Glen Garden in Fort Worth.

Hogan was ten years old when he saw his father commit suicide, and after that he sold newspapers on the street to support his family. His other home was the caddie yard and that was as tough as the street. You ought to hear Jackie Burke talk about caddie pens in Houston when his dad was a pro at River Oaks. Burke learned to shoot dice when he was ten; Hogan was rolled down hills in barrels.

Nelson had natural ability; Hogan had to work at it. He failed many times, but when he found that precision and focus he was unstoppable. Even then he had to battle back from that near-fatal car wreck and wound up winning three majors in 1953.

I played in the last tournament Hogan played—the 1971 Houston Open at Champions. I was an amateur and Hogan wrenched his left knee trying to get out of a ravine on the fourth hole. On the eleventh hole he realized he couldn't go anymore and hopped into a cart. "Don't ever get old, fellas," he said as they drove away. That was the last time he played in a tournament.

Only two players could break Hogan up—Bolt and Demaret. He was great friends with them and Demaret's partner at Champions, Jackie Burke. Around those two characters he would laugh, and you could tell he really enjoyed their company. With most everyone else he was all business.

I love the famous picture of him taken from behind at Merion. It's hanging in my office. It really says everything about him.

Nelson was nothing like Hogan. He was much more open and not nearly so reserved, which is interesting because they were so often compared to each other. Byron was a terrific player in his prime, but that prime ended at age thirty-four when he decided to walk away from the game. The decision was simple from Nelson's standpoint—he'd had enough. He always wanted to settle down on a ranch, and his first wife, Louise, felt the same way. They'd just had enough of the traveling; of driving from tournament to tournament in their cars and worrying about making enough money to eat and put tires on those cars.

Hogan was so broke at one point in 1939 he didn't have money to pay his hotel bill, someone had stolen all four of his tires, and he was about to quit. Instead he shot a closing 69 that day in Oakland, finished second, and won $380—enough to pay the bills, get new tires, and keep him going until the following year when he won his first tournament. We heard so many stories out there like that.

Nelson gave all that up for his ranch in Roanoke, Texas, which isn't far from the Dallas–Fort Worth Airport. He lives there now with his second wife, Peggy, who really gave Byron a lot of new energy at a time when he could have faded into the background. Instead, Peggy really helped him stay active in golf—and his PGA Tour event each spring—and the golf world was fortunate enough to rediscover Byron again in 1995 on the fiftieth anniversary of his eleven-tournament winning streak.

It's tough to compare eras, but when Tiger was going for his sixth straight PGA Tour victory last year, it put Nelson's streak into perspective. Even if Tiger had won that sixth at Torrey Pines—he finished second to Phil Mickelson—he still would have been only halfway to breaking Nelson's record. The only comparison I can make with Nelson's streak is Joe DiMaggio's fifty-six-game hitting streak. And Byron's was greater.

It's never too early to talk about how great Tiger can be or how great he already is. It's on everyone's mind. My jury was out when he turned pro and it was still out after he ran away with the Masters. But since then he's gone into a different dimension.

Who's the best? Nelson? Jones? Hogan? Nicklaus? Woods? You take any of the Hogans or Joneses and, if they were transported to today, they'd find a way to win now, too. But Tiger? He's doing things that have never been done before, and people are so enamored of him.

Still, I think the best way to look at it is to remember what Bobby Jones told Hogan after Hogan's ticker tape parade in New York following that British Open win.

"I think we must agree that all a man can do is beat the people who are around at the same time he is. He cannot win from those who came before any more than he can from those who may come afterward. It is grossly unfair to anyone who takes pride in the record he is able to compile that he must see it compared to those of other players who have been competing against entirely different people under wholly different conditions."

Truer words have never been spoken. And they remind me of what Nelson's record could have been.

I never really talked with Byron about his decision to just walk away, but he made it clear why he did it. When he put together his really fine years, he said, "Every time I made a birdie, that might be enough to buy another cow." So it was like building blocks. He set his goal, reached it at a young age, and became a rancher.

I never really saw him play or practice in his prime, but I watched him on film and I'd listen to Harvey talk about him. The classic argument is who was the better ball striker, Hogan or Nelson? They were both awfully good.

Hogan could command the ball with such precision. Nelson, through trial and error, figured out a swing that was right for him but which was different for that time. He tried to keep the club as low as he could, straight back away from the ball and all the way through. He was trying to make it longer through the ball because he thought he could hit the ball straighter that way. To do that you have to use your knees quite a lot, and he believed in using the legs, hips, and knees in this sort of rocking chair movement. Players who keep the ball on line the best are those who use their lower body well because the feet, the knees, are what keep the club on line. Watching him play in films, he looks like he never missed a shot.

Of course, Byron's legacy is his mind-boggling streak. I don't care who is playing, what course they're playing, or anything else. Champions still have to shoot good scores and play better than everybody else in the field. People can say all they want about the competition Byron faced because of the war years, but unbelievable players were still out there and he faced problems of travel and inconsistent equipment.

Many players can recall getting a golf ball from somebody in the gallery and playing with it as long as it would last. Things we take for granted, such as courtesy cars, all the golf balls we want, private jets, corporate outings, buffet meals at the course—players in Byron's day had none of them. So you look at his streak and wonder how he kept it going. Well, he went around in 67 or 68 every time he was on the golf course. That's amazing.

Demaret came up much the same way as Hogan and Nelson. I remember meeting him at the first tournament Dad took Charlie and me to—the 1962 Texas Open. He had a giant smile on his face—the kind that told me there had never been a bad day in his life, and that made a huge impression on me. He was friends with Dad, and when Jimmy built Onion Creek in Austin, Dad actually served as legal counsel for the formation of the club and negotiated the water rights. When I was coming up he used to tell Dad, "The kid's losing a hundred thousand dollars every year he stays in school."

Jimmy was a natural showman. He had won three Masters but you wouldn't know it. He loved people and was always making someone smile. He even launched a series of golf-to-music albums one time, of him singing with an instruction booklet. It was one of those novelty things. They didn't sell well, but I still have a few lying around the house. Jimmy was kind of an early-day Peter Jacobsen—he could sing, was witty and very funny. At times Jackie said Jimmy would tell him he'd rather sing than play golf. In fact, Jimmy had a contract singing at a nightclub in Galveston and, after he won his first Masters in 1940, he went back to Galveston for fear he might lose his job. Money wasn't the object, just a means to an end.

Jimmy kind of helped raise Jackie and in the 1960s they created Champions—a golf-only club in Houston. People thought they were crazy, but it worked. So did their partnership—Jackie ran things, Jimmy smoothed over the feathers Jackie ruffled.

Jackie's tough on people. There's forever a kid in his heart, but he's always searching for perfection. With a sense of humor, of course. He won't let anybody up. I don't care who it is—his second wife Robin, who's a fine amateur player, or his youngest daughter Meghan. He's going to be on you. He's unmerciful on me the way he teases me, but he just wants to make me understand.

I am such an easy target. Right after we won the Ryder Cup, Jackie and I were talking and he got wound up, as he usually does. "You are absolutely the miracle man! If you ever want to start a church, I'm joining! We're talking parting the Red Sea, tearing up the loaves, throwing those fishes in the basket, the Sermon on the Mount." I got the point.

He had a wonderful career, winning both the Masters and PGA in 1956, and no one has ever looked prettier standing over a putt. But when you go to the range with him, the floodgates open. He is constantly getting you ready. I know in his brain golf is Mortal Kombat.

In fact, when he was paired with someone he didn't like, he would look at the guy and say, "All right, pal, one of us is going down today and it ain't going to be me."

Jackie can be very abrasive at times but we all come to learn from him. He has been through it all and what he tells you is real. He's had the same sensations. He knows what it takes. Every time you talk to him you learn more. He leaves you with bold impressions. If he beats up on you, he's just trying to get you back on the tee. Like when someone comes in and wins, he'll remind them, "Those clubs over there don't know what you've done. You've got to get out there and start over."

And when he's down about things? He heads to the caddie shack. "I go talk to these guys for a while," he said. "It puts everything in perspective."

I learned the game from all those guys, but I never knew I could laugh so hard on a golf course until I played a practice round with Lee Trevino and Chi Chi Rodriguez. Lee nudged me and said, "Watch this." He took a jar of jalapeños out of his bag and went over to a woman in the gallery. "Little lady, do you want some candy?" he asked.

She ate it and ran straight to the water fountain. Lee and Chi Chi were rolling on the ground laughing on the tee box. Lee finally went over and helped her and she laughed, too. Lee was pulling stuff like that all the time—like when he threw that rubber snake at Jack on the first hole of the 1971 Open playoff at Merion.

Lee went on to win that Open, too, beating Jack by three shots. There was nothing funny about that—or the other five majors he won—but there was plenty funny about Trevino. He could get away with a lot of things that none of the rest of us could, like that week when, during a practice round, he was in the rough with a pith helmet on, carrying a hatchet and that rubber snake.

Trevino had a flat swing, a strong grip, started the club a little bit outside, swung in, and cut the ball like you've never seen. Of course, he loved playing in the wind because he hit this low ball. Part of what gave

Trevino his nerve was his upbringing, when he was hustling on the golf course to make a little money. It hardened him and he learned how to compete. And, like Hogan, he saw a lot of things while growing up, not all of them pretty. He always said that the toughest way to play golf is to bet somebody when you don't have the money in your pocket. He's right.

Texans have really been a fraternity on the Tour. We know we're a part of a great tradition and have a lot to live up to. We spend a lot of time with each other, which should come as no surprise. In the '80s, Bruce Lietzke and I used to play practice rounds against Miller Barber and Don January, and they were some of the most fun rounds I ever played. And any bets? At least the money stayed in Texas.

I could go on about Texans forever—Ralph Guldahl who quit to sell cars, then came back to win two U.S. Opens, in 1937 and 1938, and the 1939 Masters; dashing Lloyd Mangrum, an early-day Palmer who won thirty-six tournaments including the 1946 U.S. Open; legends like Titanic Thompson and Lefty Stackhouse; my buddies Leaky and Buck; Tom Kite and Justin Leonard, who hasn't reached thirty yet but already owns a British Open title.

Texas proud? You bet we are. Whether it's a Tour event, a whirlwind round with former President George Bush, a lazy afternoon with Willie and Coach Royal, or a quick visit with Byron or Jackie, we've all got a bond, a legacy. And we can't wait to see how the next generation enhances it.

10.

PEAKS AND VALLEYS

TOUGHEST THINGS ABOUT
THE PGA TOUR

Losing a playoff
Missing the cut
Travel
Rain delays
A late tee time with a lead
Early-morning tee times out West
(frosty!)

Bill Hooten, one of my good friends from Dallas, wanted to see Salem Country Club so we decided to take a tour one morning. Well, I guess I should clarify—the morning of the final round of the 1988 U.S. Open.

I was playing late, maybe three groups from the end that year at Brookline, and we figured we could get to Salem and back in plenty of time. Of course, we weren't quite sure how to get back, even if it was only about twenty miles north of Boston, so when we finally pulled into the parking lot Julie was there tapping her foot.

"Where have you guys been?" she demanded. "Don't you know this is the U.S. Open?"

I have a pitiful habit of doing things like that. It's not that I don't care, it's just that I get caught up from time to time. But even though I did cut it close, I shot my low round of the week—a 67—and tied for twelfth.

I swear Julie's still mad at me about that one. But that's just me.

And, it's a pretty good window into my career.

I was playing well that week, so no matter how many crazy things I did, I was still going to have a decent finish. But that wasn't always the case.

Over the years I've had more peaks and valleys than I care to count. Ben Crenshaw on a smooth, even keel? No way. Not ever.

Sure, I've had some incredibly wonderful moments—more than I could have ever imagined—but I also fell into some pretty deep pits. If those holes had been much steeper, I'm not sure I could have gotten out of them without someone throwing me a long rope. And when I was at my lowest, I really didn't have much confidence in what I was doing—or what I was trying to do.

This game will get you down, there is no doubt about it. If it hasn't got you yet, it will. It's coming. The key is in how you handle it. Of course, it's taken me fifty years and help from Dave Marr to figure it out.

I can't tell you how many times Dave would be talking about me on a telecast and say, "Ben is on his twenty-first comeback now." He made me laugh, which wasn't always the easiest thing to do.

My two biggest wins—my two Masters—both came just after some gut-wrenching times. The first one came just after my decision to end my first marriage; the second a week after Harvey died. Both times I somehow found a peace and strength that pulled me out of the valleys. But it wasn't always that way. There were times when I stayed in those valleys a long while.

One of the highest points in my life came in 1985. So did one of the lowest.

We met on the twelfth hole at Riviera. She had on a light-blue tennis dress and was the cutest thing I ever saw. I'll certainly confess I wasn't looking for a wife, seeing as how I was still trying to overcome an unhappy marriage, and told her just that. Even so, we agreed to have a date a month later. It was the best date I ever made.

Julie and I had a long-distance courtship—first with her in Los Angeles, then in Dallas when she went through American Airlines flight attendant school—but even though we had our trials and tribulations, it was clear to me she was the one. We married that November at the Kapalua Invitational and, yes, the invitation list was filled with caddies and players.

Julie took right to my life. She didn't know anything about golf—she laughs about when she heard I'd won the Masters and said, "Isn't that nice?"—but she picked right up on it. She's very competitive, full of spirit and determination. A few people close to me weren't fired up about the relationship, let alone the marriage, but as time went by they understood how much she loved me, how much she meant to me, and how I confided everything with her. Marrying her is the best decision I've ever made in my life.

I don't want to sound sappy, but when you find somebody that you love in every way—spiritually and emotionally—it completes a circle in your life. She has given me a reason to live and she's given me three of the most beautiful daughters you've ever seen—Katherine, Claire, and Anna Riley. The only males in the house are me and the cat B. J., short for Bobby Jones.

I don't know what I would have done without her that first year. When I was going through the divorce, the stress triggered a thyroid problem that had me baffled for quite a while. I had gone through low times with my swing before—most notably in 1982 when it felt as though it was in a hundred different pieces. With the help of Harvey and college teammate Brent Buckman, I finally worked my way out of that even while my personal life was a mess. But this health problem was tougher.

At first the symptoms were kind of baffling. I started losing weight and my heart got to beating very fast and irregularly. I was very winded, weak, and had difficulty sleeping. I'd get to sleep fine but wake back up. And I was always hot, constantly turning the air conditioner down. All kinds of things were going on that weren't right.

And I wasn't playing worth a darn from the end of 1984 through all of 1985. I couldn't even chip. I lost my touch completely.

Everybody kept telling me I'd lost a ton of weight, but I tried to put it out of my mind. I kept rationalizing it, telling myself that if I could just have a good week, I could get back. Finally in November 1985, I had a routine insurance exam.

"Have you had your thyroid checked?" the doctor asked. I hadn't, so he ran the tests.

Sure enough, they revealed that my thyroid was tremendously overactive—I had what they called Graves disease—so I went to the nuclear medicine department at the University of Texas. They gave me a dose of radioactive iodine and I started feeling better a month later. I started taking synthetic thyroid medicine and it was amazing. Although we didn't get everything right until April 1986, I started gaining weight and began to get my touch and confidence back—all because of swallowing that iodine, which tasted like metal.

Things began to turn around in June, when I contended at the U.S. Open at Shinnecock. Going into the back nine on Sunday, I was one of twelve players tied for the lead and wound up finishing sixth behind Raymond. That tournament—coupled with the iodine, Julie, and Scotty—triggered one of the most successful, consistent periods in my career. Later that summer I won the Buick Open, then the Vantage Championship in the fall. I won twice more in the next two years—at New Orleans and Doral—and finished in the top eight on the money list all three of those years.

Just as Julie came into my life, I was also making a management change. After years of being represented by International Management Group, I decided I wanted a Texas-based manager. I ran it past Scotty, a lifelong friend—we go all the way back to those Little League teams Dad coached—and he said he'd love to take a shot at it. He'd been in other businesses, and I didn't have to think too long. He jumped right in and started handling the business aspect of my life.

He's been fantastic. He's my best friend, he gave me peace of mind, and he turned up more meaningful business for me than IMG had. He's his own man—very smart and quick—and has been a real blessing, helping me with everything from the Graves disease to my architecture business, the Ryder Cup, and this book.

I was so thankful to finally understand what had made me feel so bad. It's funny how one little gland in your neck can be so important, but it is. The tough thing was I was in the public eye through the whole thyroid ordeal. At almost every tournament I played, reporters were asking questions about my health. There were also rumors that I was on hard drugs. That was ridiculous and hurt me terribly at a time when I was simply trying to get healthy.

It wasn't always easy, but that's one of the things you accept as a professional athlete. I knew that a lot of people out there—people outside my family and circle of close friends—cared about me and wanted to see me get well.

I'm in one of those valleys now. The Ryder Cup was such a high, with so many emotions, but I haven't been playing well for a while now. I'm hoping it's just one of those times every player seems to go through as he gets older. I'm hoping it will turn around soon; I'm looking forward to getting my enthusiasm back.

People ask me if I feel I did all I could on the PGA Tour. I don't know. I may look at things a little differently now.

As I was playing, I knew I was capable of winning and of winning major tournaments. I suppose you have to look inside yourself and ask, "Are you as good as they say? Or as good as some people close to you hope you can be?" But, at the end of the day, you've got to say to yourself, "I am capable and I have achieved what I thought I could achieve."

In looking back, yes, I was a good player—a darned good player. But however you want to define good and great, there's a vast gulf between the two, and I'd be in the good category. I wasn't a great player. Great players have more, sharper points in their game that serve them in good stead in many places in many competitions.

Did I strive many times to get better? Absolutely. I don't think people will understand that many times I suffered over getting better and never could figure it out as well or as consistently as some other players could. And I finally resigned myself to saying that the more technical, more precise I tried to get, the worse I'd play. I'd go backwards. And the times I would really play well? I would just play. I would play a lot and play a lot of rounds. I just couldn't unlock the secret of getting appreciably better. I couldn't get my game consistent enough to be in a position to win tournaments. I wish I had been able to develop that consistency.

Like Dave said, I was always on a comeback. He would say, "He's fired and fallen back as much as any player." There's a lot of truth to that.

I couldn't resign myself to that when I was playing a lot. Young golfers are restless to get better and they'll do anything to improve. So many times in practice sessions I would go out and hit balls and hit balls. I'd ask myself, what have I gotten out of this? Am I on the right track? Am I getting better? Do I have something to hang my hat on? And usually the answer was no.

Over the last twenty-nine years I've accomplished a lot of things. I've won nineteen times on tour, including two majors and three other times worldwide. I've lost eight playoffs, which shows I approached the winner's circle eight more times and didn't get in. And you know what? I'm okay with that.

It's easy to accept when you read what Jones wrote: "There's more to life than winning tournaments."

In the end, he's right.

11.

A WINDOW
TO THE SOUL

FAVORITE GOLF COURSE
ARCHITECTS

Alister MacKenzie
Donald Ross
A. W. Tillinghast
C. B. Macdonald
George Thomas
Perry Maxwell
Seth Raynor
Harry Colt

It's been said that if St. Andrews hadn't been christened the cradle of golf, it would be just another course.

That's not right.

It's a wonderful course with a special atmosphere that pervades everything because of the Scottish people. That golf ground is like an extension of their being—the links and the townspeople are synonymous. It's their golf course, it's their land; their place for recreation—for who knows how many centuries.

They're very plain, very honest, churchgoing people, and because of that and the fact that St. Andrews is the ecclesiastical seat of Scotland, it's almost like going onto holy ground. For them, St. Andrews can be a round of golf or just a nice walk. They can contemplate things. They just roam. It's anything but formal.

And the course itself? It's totally natural. In fact, very few things have been done to it. Old Tom Morris and Allan Robertson were the real curators of the Old Course, but essentially all they did was prepare the ground for play.

I've spent hours wandering there, playing the course, studying the way it was carved by nature. The Old Course gets better the more you play it. It's endlessly fascinating, changing with every shift in the breeze, but there's always a way to play it. You're not dictated the way you are on so many courses today. And the contours of the greens are incredible, multiplying what can happen to the ball. There are no perfect bounces here. You get some good breaks, you get some bad breaks. Just imagine how dull it would be if we always knew what was going to happen to the ball.

The Old Course violates a lot of today's architectural acceptances—it has crossfire holes, it presents traffic problems going out and back, and you're slowed by the double greens. But Dr. MacKenzie always wanted architecture students to go there and study—especially the ladies' putting green. It's incredible to see all of the undulations.

I've always liked that quirky architecture. I like the freedom, the movement. I don't like being dictated how to play a hole, and St. Andrews gives golfers many options. Your hands are so full, and you just tackle it. It's literally like an outdoor chess game.

One of the courses I built with Bill Coore—Sand Hills in Nebraska—is a links-style course with elevation change. Still, you'll see that Bill and I applied a lot of what we learned about St. Andrews there.

Architecture and history have been my passions since that first day I saw The Country Club and started to understand everything I'd read in Charles Price's book. Seeing a totally unique golf course for the first time, seeing a totally different topography, I was hooked. It was so beautiful—natural, craggy—and I was captivated by the use of different grasses of different colors and textures. It all fit beautifully and in proportion. I haven't stopped studying since.

More often than not, Julie will walk through my library and I'll have my nose stuck in a book. I didn't get a college degree in golf course architecture, but I have studied it and prepared as hard as others prepare for other careers.

People will say it's easy to build a golf hole, but it's not. If you haven't studied the great golf holes and where things are most apt to go in a natural setting, if you don't have a sense of an idea and proportion and balance, you can't do it. Architecture is a million things rolled into one hole, one course. It's the study of agronomy, science, geography, artwork, and sculpture because you're sculpting land on the biggest canvas you can imagine. It is tremendously creative, tremendously rewarding, tremendously fulfilling. I get every bit as much fun out of building a course as playing, and I'm very lucky to be able to do both.

I've talked about 1985 as being a turning point in my personal life. It was also the year I launched my career in course architecture.

Another blessing in my life was meeting Bill Coore. He's very wise, very patient, very methodical, and, while he is an extension of my philosophy, he has also guided me. He sees the practical side of building a golf hole and sees it through a golf course superintendent's eyes.

Bill and I met one day when I was looking at a potential project in Corpus Christi. Bill, who went to work with Pete Dye after graduating from Wake Forest, built nearby Rockport Country Club and happened to drop by. We met, went to see his course, and I really liked what I saw. I called him later, but he wasn't thinking about a partnership. A lot of conversations later we teamed up.

As Bill said when we first started, "If we treat this as a hobby we can always have fun at it." He was right.

Our first two projects were renovating all eighteen greens at Houston Country Club and the first and second greens at Prairie Dunes in Hutchinson, Kansas. We weren't in any hurry and didn't want to work on more than one or two projects at once, and after a few false starts and canceled projects we built The Plantation Course at Kapalua and the Cliffside Course at Barton Creek Country Club in Austin.

Our crews have been with us since the start and we try to pursue only projects where we can put our best foot forward, which means taking a piece of land that reflects a sense of golf and doing little things in order to bring the holes out. We do rudimentary blueprints, but we like to be outside and work on details in the field. And, we pick projects where golf is at the forefront. We would not be inclined to take a project where we saw golf taking a back seat to any kind of development. If golf is going to be showcased, then we're interested. If it's a good piece of land, we're interested. If they're good people whom we think we can get along with and share our interests, we're interested.

Like St. Andrews, we want our courses to be fun and interesting for all classes of golfers. And we always like to set a golf course down quietly in its surroundings, leaving it with a natural look.

No matter what we build in the future, I think Sand Hills will always be our favorite. Dick Youngscap, who had the vision for Sand Hills, opened our eyes to a part of the country that is beautiful, natural, and perfectly suited to golf. When you play there, you have to plan shots in advance and you have to play shots not only in the air but on the ground. It reflects solitude and was one of the most inspiring projects we will ever have.

When I saw the land for the first time, I couldn't believe it. There are fifteen thousand square miles of sand hills in Nebraska, and it took a year to route the holes. The land was so good we couldn't decide what direction to go. In the end we designed a links course—at thirty-six hundred feet above sea level—so, much like playing in Denver, the ball goes a long way.

Coore-Crenshaw has had many great experiences, but one important job that didn't turn out as we would have liked was at Riviera Country Club, when we restored the greens and bunkers to get them ready for the 1995 PGA Championship. Things didn't turn out as planned.

The USGA had wanted Riviera to redo the greens because they were not draining well. We rebuilt the greens under USGA specifications, but instead of seeding the greens, Riviera decided to sod them. Unfortunately the roots never took hold, and it was evident six months before the PGA when the Nissan Open was held there.

My heart sank. It wasn't going as planned and we knew we had to shoulder the blame. It was painful for everybody, including the Riviera management and members—and even to the memory of George Thomas, the architect of Riviera. It meant a great deal to us to do that job correctly. We did it and it didn't work.

During the PGA some of the greens were simply not strong enough. What grass there was had to be cut short for speed, but that compounded the problem. After the tournament, Paul Latshaw, one of country's best superintendents, stepped in and brought the greens back.

Since then we have been involved with several projects including Cuscowilla, halfway between Atlanta and Augusta; the Warren Golf Course at Notre Dame; East Hampton Golf Club; Chechessee Creek Golf Club in South Carolina, Hidden Creek in New Jersey, Friar's Head in Long Island, and Austin Golf Club right here at home.

I've been blessed beyond belief to see the world's greatest courses. I honestly get very excited when I get near one of these courses because I'm going to have the chance to study it. I think a magnificent course reveals its highlights and secrets to you over a lifetime. If there are different things about it that you observe every day, then it's a pretty enthralling piece of work. But if you pick it up in no time and you don't learn anything about it, the golf course isn't what it should be.

My library continues to be one of my great treasures. People from the British Isles have been so generous, giving me so many books no one in their families wanted. I think three-quarters of my collection is British or Scottish and that's influenced me so much. Who knows exactly when golf started, but we do know that the terrain in Scotland is perfectly suited for golf. The game started on land that couldn't be used for agriculture and was almost regarded as throwaway land. The grass was close-growing and had a springy quality and the people had the good sense to leave it alone. A lot of times they let their hazards be formed by wind or animals.

I do love St. Andrews, but my heart belongs to Augusta National. I've had a lot of cherished moments there, but, as I've said so many times, that golf course is a wonder to itself. It's about as beautiful a piece of terrain as you could ever want to see. And Bob Jones and Dr. MacKenzie let the beauty of the course stand alone.

Other favorites of mine are Merion, Pine Valley, Pinehurst, The National Golf Links, Shinnecock, Winged Foot, Riviera, Cypress Point, and Pebble Beach. Each architect of those courses left their beliefs and stamp on them. I also love Royal Melbourne, in the sand belt region of Melbourne—one of the greatest pieces of terrain on earth. Australians know how to take care of their courses, staying on the lean side, conserving water, and taking care of their native grasses.

As far as architects, Tom Fazio and Pete Dye and the Jones family—Robert Trent Jones Sr., Rees, and Robert Trent Jones Jr.—have all done outstanding work as have player-architects Jack and Arnold. They do volume, which is not to say that they have done shoddy work, because they bring golfers a fine product. Of the player-architects coming up now, Greg Norman is starting to do good work, and Tom Weiskopf is maybe one of the most serious guys about the business.

I don't judge a course by the name on it. I like to see fine golf courses and great art. And golf course architecture is art.

You couldn't learn everything there is to know about it in a lifetime of study. It's all part and parcel of the learning experience and, like golfers, architects learn more from their mistakes than their successes.

The bottom line is, you're judged by your work. Whether it's ten, twenty, thirty, forty, or fifty years out, you leave an imprint. You leave a bit of your philosophy behind when you build a golf course. It's a part of you and, in some ways, a reflection of the way you treat people. The easiest thing in the world is to build a hard golf course. It's far harder to design a golf course that's playable for everyone.

Dr. MacKenzie said a course cannot be judged as a good course unless it's playable for all golfers, regardless of handicap. We think about that all the time. The entrances to the greens are how you treat people; the courses themselves an opportunity to allow everyone to enjoy a round.

We hope our courses, like Dr. MacKenzie's and others, will be seen as windows to our souls.

12.

THE FIFTEENTH CLUB

<table>
<tr><td>

THINGS A GOLFER NEEDS
WHEN PLAYING
AUGUSTA NATIONAL

Feel
Touch
Imagination
Instinct
Nerves
Patience
Emotion
Bravery
Trust
A good caddie

</td></tr>
</table>

The message came while Julie and I were enjoying a quiet dinner in the Trophy Room Sunday night. Maitre d' Arthur Williams handed Julie the slip of paper—"Call Tom or Christy Kite" it read—and she knew what had happened. She slipped out, called Christy to get the details, and then called me away from our dinner companions—Masters chairman Jack Stephens and Pat Summerall.

Julie wasn't going to let me hear it on the phone, so we walked out to the porch and she told me Harvey had died. As much as we had prepared for that moment, it still hit us hard. We stood there and cried a bit and talked for about fifteen minutes. She asked if I wanted to go home, but I didn't. I wanted to be with friends, so we stayed. Inside, Mr. Stephens and Pat weren't sure what to say, but that was fine. They let me talk about Harvey—what he'd meant to me, my family, and golf. I reminisced and they laughed. It was a wonderful way to celebrate his life.

When I got back to the house I talked to Tom, who was standing on Harvey's porch, helping to make phone calls. He had come up with a plan—he would fly over Monday, get a practice round in, then we would all fly back to the funeral in Austin on Wednesday. We talked for a few minutes and when we hung up, I cried again.

Looking back now, I could see things beginning to unfold. Every time any of us left Austin, we knew there was a chance Harvey wouldn't be there when we returned. No one wanted to be gone when it happened. I was, but maybe that helped me. I was away from the emotions in Austin and could deal with my feelings—and mine alone.

I thought back to our final visit; the day Julie, Katherine, and Claire had played with Helen and Bud Shrake while I was getting that lesson from Harvey. He had never recovered from a bout with pneumonia and seemed in so much pain. He was getting weaker. I put my hand on his, kissed his forehead, and said, "I love you, Harvey."

He looked at me and said, "I love you, too, Ben."

I couldn't believe he was gone.

When Carl arrived at the course Monday morning he didn't know what to expect. He'd been beside me at Augusta for some twenty years—ever since John Griffith had introduced us. Carl had been Jack Stephens' caddie forever. He's a soft-spoken man; a very caring man.

He had to be wondering if I would be able to concentrate. If I could put Harvey's death behind me. If the two of us would be able to right what was wrong.

A few swings into that first practice round, Carl saw the problem. I was reaching at the ball and I continued doing it through a post-round visit to the range. But Carl, being Carl, waited for the right moment to bring it up. He found it the next morning.

He was standing behind me on the range and told me I had the ball a bit too far up in my stance and my shoulder turn was a bit looser than usual. I hit four balls, knew I'd found something, and told Carl that was surely the best practice session I'd had in a long while.

So much was unspoken that week. Carl knew what I was going through. We had formed a friendship, a bond, over the years as Carl guided me across a course we both loved. He can read me so well. He knew what I needed; he knew what to do.

I wasn't the only one struggling. Tom was upset and so was Davis Love, who had played his way into the field by winning in New Orleans just minutes before Harvey died. His father had been a devoted pupil of Harvey's and he was torn about flying to the funeral. Tom and I convinced him to stay behind and work on his game, reminding him that he was playing great and had as much chance to win as anyone. That's what his dad would have told him, too.

Little did I know what the next few days would bring.

Tom, Christy, Julie, Chuck Cook, Terry Jastrow, and I made the two-and-a-half-hour flight to Austin Wednesday morning where we were greeted by gray, rainy skies for the funeral. Tom and I were both pallbearers and when the service was over, both Dad and Charlie told me there was a peace surrounding me that they had never seen. I hugged them both before we left and told them I was onto something. They said there was a twinkle in my eye and conviction in my voice. I wouldn't realize it until later. I was thinking about Harvey.

When you think about someone who meant so much to your life, you think about all the times and all the things he taught us—you try to absorb as much as you can. In a lot of ways it was a very appropriate time for him to go, a week when he would be on everyone's mind.

And I would feel his hand resting on my shoulder.

Tom and I slept most of the way back, and after heading our separate ways from the airport we both found our way out to the course. Davis was still practicing when I got there and Tom had already rushed to the practice tee. I hit a few balls, then went to the putting green and tried three putters—Little Ben; a Cleveland Classic 8802 clone that belonged to Scotty, and a black 8802. I didn't decide which one to use until later that night when, after swinging them all again that night in the house, I settled on Scotty's putter, which Julie immediately nicknamed "Little Scotty."

That same rainy front followed us, settling on Augusta Thursday morning. I didn't let that or a difficult round by playing partner Ian Baker-Finch get me down. Instead I was focused. I had taken Carl's suggestions to heart—they were the same observations Harvey would have made if he'd been there—and I was trusting my swing again.

The spark was there once again.

I was working on something positive—hitting a lot of shots with authority and making some putts. And nothing helps your confidence more than seeing yourself do what you're trying to do. So when I bogeyed the first hole I shrugged it off. I wasn't distracted by Ian's 79, although I later found out we came dangerously close to a slow-play warning at Amen Corner.

I saw rules official Judy Bell, the USGA president at the time, at the twelfth and said hello, but she didn't come over to chat. I later found out that she saw I was a bit distracted and didn't want me to stop and talk and risk a penalty.

I enjoyed that round and opened with a 70, four back of the leaders. I could feel the shots. I was playing the course. And that night, as always, we threw our annual barbecue—for all ten people staying in the five-bedroom rental house, a few more close personal and corporate friends, like Bob Coletta and Jim McGovern from Buick, C. J. McDaniel, who runs Crenshaw Golf, and Jeff Rose and Preston Piermattei, who were with Bobby Jones at the time. Rob Gillette, the head of Ben's Battalion, was there, and as usual brought along an etched bottle of wine. Eventually he only stayed through the third round. Why? He'd promised his wife he'd be home to teach Sunday school. I think he's still kicking himself.

We enjoyed ourselves, but it had already been a long week, so we were in bed by 10 P.M.

By Friday, Team Crenshaw was beginning to feel pretty good

about what they saw me doing. My close friend Pat Oles, an Austin developer, was in charge of grabbing the best viewing spot on every hole and keeping an eye out for potential trouble. Julie called him "the Advance Man." I called him Rommel—the field general. It really was fun to hear about how he'd scurry through crowds and post up at the greens to get a clear view, but he did get me a little upset at the ninth hole when I hit a huge drive that seemed destined for the pine trees on the left.

Pat took off running and beat me to the ball. When I saw him sprinting, I asked Carl if there was something wrong with the shot. There wasn't. I gave Pat a hard look and he slowed down after that.

If there was a turning point to the week, it came at fourteen. Only a few writers picked up on it—those who'd talked to Carl and me—but it was huge. I had an over-the-hill, around-the-break, to-the-back-of-the-green, we-weren't-sure-we-read-it-right forty-five-foot putt. It was so tough it could easily have been a four-putt. But I studied it and lagged it to eighteen inches.

Carl was shaking his head as he walked past Julie. "That," he said, "was the meanest putt I've ever seen."

By the end of the day my 67 left me two behind Jay Haas, who shot a fabulous 64. I was beginning to get a feeling. Everything felt seamless. I was playing steady, smooth golf. Little mistakes I made were erased quickly. Things were coming together.

I was taking dead aim.

I began to think I might be there at the end, because all I wanted to do was be there with a chance. That's anyone's goal going there. It was too difficult to think about what would happen if. I was just trying to play like Harvey wanted me to.

That night, calls began coming in from friends. Kurt and Janice Haney, Knox Fitzpatrick, Bob Kinnan, Martin Davis, Robert MacDonald, Billy Munn, Bobby Kay, Bill Hooten, Brent and Ed Clements all called to wish me luck. I spoke with Julie's parents and I had a long talk with Dad. He wasn't able to walk around Augusta any longer. The hills were just too high, but Scotty called him from each concession stand on the course to keep him posted on my progress. He was there with me in spirit.

I finished the third round tied for the lead with Brian Henninger—a shot better than what felt like half the field. Fred Couples, Phil Mickelson, Steve Elkington, Jay Haas and Scott Hoch were tied right behind us, Curtis Strange, David Frost, and John Huston were only two shots back, and Greg Norman and Davis were just three back. That meant that an even dozen players—including some of the best in the world—were within three shots of each other. The leaderboard was absolutely stacked; this Masters could belong to anyone up there. It was up for grabs.

While I was talking to the press that night, Julie called Charlie in Austin and told him to be on the next plane to Augusta. Charlie had missed my win in 1984 and Julie didn't want him to miss this one.

Like I said earlier, the hardest thing about being in contention at a major is the wait. It's interminable. No one tees off until close to 2 P.M., and no one can sleep past 10.

I was out on the lawn chipping pine cones when Charlie arrived around noon. Everyone was taking turns and he joined in. We talked for a while and I remember smiling at him and saying, "Let's go see what happens."

Not long after that I stopped in mid-thought and walked down the driveway. I was lost. I tried pondering the day and just let myself relax, allowing the peace I was feeling to wash across me. I thought about Harvey. Somehow, I knew he would be with me.

Preston Piermattei, who was in charge of my wardrobe for the week, stopped by and suggested that I wear a shirt that had images of Bobby Jones winning the four legs of the Grand Slam in 1930. It seemed appropriate for the final day of this tournament.

Things started happening quickly that afternoon. I pulled my tee shot at the second hole, but the ball hit a limb and dropped harmlessly to the edge of the fairway and I made birdie. "A Harvey bounce," Julie said.

I did bogey the fifth, but I stiffed my tee shot at the sixth and saved par from the back bunker at the seventh. Then I gambled at the ninth, stiffed that approach for birdie, and made the turn at two-under.

I just kept thinking: "Play each hole. Take what the course gives you. Feel the shot. Don't let anything come into your mind except those two things you're working on. And trust yourself."

Carl and I have always had a saying there—"It's time to reach deep." When we made the turn we didn't have to say it. We could see it in each other's eyes.

I've always been one to watch leaderboards, but that day I didn't look until the back nine. I knew I was leading because of the crowd reaction and I knew I was playing well. Most of the other players had fallen back, and when I looked at the board after fifteen, I saw I was tied with Davis, who was already in the scoring tent with a 66. I had three holes left. That meant I had to make one more birdie.

Usually it's the guy who finishes first in a situation like that who wins. But not this time.

There wasn't a question in my mind when I stepped to the sixteenth tee. I saw a crystal-clear 6-iron with a hint of a draw that was working its way toward the hole. I got that birdie.

At the seventeenth I hit a 9-iron to thirteen feet and made an improbable left-to-right putt for another birdie—and a two-shot lead. Then I pulled out a 4-wood at the eighteenth and let it rip.

My heart was pounding. I started out and all of a sudden it was like, I can't believe this. This week, these circumstances, this man who gave me my life in golf. How could a guy be so lucky? I couldn't believe it. And I couldn't believe I was playing the kind of golf you dream of. I didn't count bogeys until later, but I only had five all week. And I'd never played a major tournament before with just five bogeys.

There was a lump in my throat when I walked off the tee and all I could hear were the cheers. I couldn't hold it in. I was already brushing away the tears.

Then I caught myself and said, "Wait a minute. I've got one more shot here."

But saying it and hitting it? It wasn't that easy. I came out of the 8-iron shot and it was short. I have to confess, I was not in good shape hitting the second shot. I was just mentally starting to break.

When that last putt dropped, I dropped. I still get a lump in my throat when I talk about it. It was such a relief that it was over and I was thinking of so many things. I was thinking of the little guy starting out in golf, of Harvey, and my family. And, I was thinking I was lucky. Carl literally had to peel me off the floor.

"Are you all right?" he asked, walking toward me.

He steadied me. That shows you the way he is—he's just a tender, tender man. I was happy for him; very proud for him. He's guided me around there so many times and there he was picking me up off the deck. I love Carl Jackson.

Once my card was signed, I saw Julie and Charlie crying behind the tent. We all hugged and cried at the back of that eighteenth hole and I'll never have a better hug in my life than when I hugged Julie. We just stood there and trembled together. We couldn't believe what had happened and that we'd gotten through such an emotional week. The second-best hug came from Charlie. We were bound so much through Harvey. He, as much as anyone, understood.

So did Carl.

"I've waited twenty years for Ben to play that well," he told Scotty as they drove toward the clubhouse in a golf cart.

"What about 1984?" he asked.

Carl smiled and shook his head. "Not even close."

We walked through the ceremonies, the interviews, the press room. And once that was done we joined the Augusta members for a quick dinner, filled with toasts and more tears. We didn't eat much.

Julie and I just held hands under the table. We were still in shock. It was the first major we won together.

Davis, who had flown home, called during the dinner to congratulate me. "I'm thrilled you won," he said. "I know Harvey's happy, too." And I got a message from Helen Penick—"Harvey and Helen send congratulations and love on this special day."

Our plane had to be in the air before 11 P.M., so we had to rush to the airport. I called Helen from the plane to say thank you.

I didn't sleep much that night and was up before six. After I made coffee, I drove to the supermarket to get a paper and came back with a grocery sack filled with papers from all around the state.

And, yes, I was crying. I was exhausted, thankful, and still floating as if it had all been a dream.

13.

PERFECT TIMING

THINGS A RYDER CUP
CAPTAIN MUST DO

Listen to his players
Make pairings
Go with your instinct
Be yourself
Make sure the players are
comfortable

It was late in the season and I was coaching first base at one of Katherine's kickball games. She hadn't played much then, but she singled and was so excited. There she was, standing a few feet from me, ready to fly down to second the first chance she got.

The next kicker was at the plate. I remember that much. The next thing I know, Katherine's been doubled off. She's out by thirty steps. She never tagged up.

"Dad, why didn't you tell me?" she said, stalking back to the dugout. She just looked at me in pity as if to say, "You dolt." It was a look that said you're incapable of being my father right now.

I hear Julie screaming at me from the stands. And Scotty, who's coaching third, is giving me a look that could kill. The pitcher had caught the pop fly and I didn't know. I wasn't paying attention; I was frozen. So how could I have told Katherine to tag up?

I stared at the ground.

When the inning was over, Scotty walked past me. "What in the world were you doing?" he said in utter disbelief.

"I was thinking about the twelfth hole at Brookline," I said. "It has that extra-tall pin because it's hidden in the blind green. I was thinking about how to play that."

I had only accepted the job as Ryder Cup captain twenty-four hours before and was already becoming obsessed with it. And with the notion that I was getting the chance of a lifetime to captain a team at the very place that had opened my eyes and heart to every aspect of the game.

It's been more than a year since that magnificent week in Brookline and I have to admit I'm still recovering from it. All of it. Physically and emotionally.

For the better part of two years I never really stopped thinking about the Ryder Cup. There were times when I could put it back on the to-do list for a while, but I just had to thrust myself into the role. I started talking to other captains, picking their brains for everything from logistics to tiny details. PGA of America public relations and media relations director Julius Mason's phone number was on my speed dial. And I thanked God for allies like Julius at the PGA and Julie and Scotty at home.

The PGA knows what they want, they know how to present it, and they know how to put it on. They've got the plans ready, and the captain slides into them and starts making that team his own.

And at home? Julie and Scotty run my life. They're so organized that whenever I would lay my head on the pillow at night and think about pairings, I would always think about them. They were always there, ready to soothe my feelings and take care of organizational details. As everyone knows, I'm not a great detail person. One of Julie's most frequent lines has always been, "Earth to Ben."

Harvey was at the airport to meet Dad and me following the 1984 Masters.
(Tammy Buckman)

Tom and I left the Masters to fly back to Austin for Harvey's funeral.
(Ralph Barrera, "Austin American Statesman")

Chipping pinecones and killing time! Sunday
morning in Augusta, 1995. *(Julie Sayers)*

"Team Crenshaw" in Augusta before the final round in 1995. *(from left)* Charlie
Crenshaw, Scotty and Julie Sayers, Julie and Pat Oles, Mary Beth Ryan, me,
and Julie. *(Amy Garrigan)*

The birdie I made on number seventeen gave me an
"extra stroke" in hand going to the final hole. It turned
out that I needed it. *(Fred Vuich)*

Jose Maria Olazabal helps me into the green jacket. *(Fred Vuich)*

Julie and I were honored to be invited to Kennebunkport prior to the Ryder Cup matches. Jaime Patino is pictured with Julie, former President Bush, and me. *(The Crenshaw Family Archives)*

Sharing a light moment with Captain James on the way to the opening ceremonies. *(Julie Crenshaw)*

Working against the Friday noon pairings deadline with assistants
Bill Rogers and Bruce Lietzke. *(Scotty Sayers)*

With Linn Strickler, Bruce Edwards, and Bill Rogers.
(Scotty Sayers)

There is a tremendous difference between participating in the Ryder Cup
matches as a player and as the captain.
As a player at the 1995 matches at Oak Hill. *(Zeke McCabe)*

As captain at The Country Club. *(Jules Alexander)*

My friends former President Bush and President George W. Bush have a family tradition rich in golf. They had a great time watching the matches at Brookline. *(Jim Mahoney, "Boston Herald")*

I had no idea that Helen Penick was at Brookline until she was brought into the team room on Sunday. A part of Harvey really was with me that day. *(Carol Grigsby)*

Celebrating with my daughter Katherine. I was so glad she could be there. *(Tom Miller)*

Victory!
(*Simon Bruty, "Sports Illustrated"*)

(*Robert Beck, "Sports Illustrated"*)

This one speaks for itself.
(Bob Martin, "Sports Illustrated")

The caddies' gift of Bob Pack's bronze rendition of Francis Ouimet and Eddie Lowery was a complete surprise, and most touching. They were a big part of our victory. *(Frank Christian)*

On the *Tonight Show* set with Jay Leno, Justin, Steve, Phil, and "The Shirt." *(Courtesy of the "Tonight Show")*

With my friends Willie Nelson and Darrell Royal. Our Ben, Willie, and Darrell tournament in Austin is always a great time and has raised more than $4,000,000 for Austin youth charities. *(Rick Henson)*

With fellow Austinite Lance Armstrong and Charles Barkley.
(Courtesy of Dan Napier, MGM Grand Hotel)

Payne Stewart was the "perfect" teammate, and always enjoyed a hard-earned victory. *(Jim Mahoney, "Boston Herald")*

Julie and I with the President-Elect, Laura Bush, and Julie and Scotty Sayers at the Governor's Mansion following his acceptance speech on December 13, 2000. *(Ron Weiss)*

Our wedding day in 1985 at Kapalua. *(The Crenshaw Family Archives)*

Finally, a chance to relax following the Ryder Cup (Venice, 2000).
(The Crenshaw Family Archives)

Dad, Charlie, and I (Christmas, 1994). We lost Dad in 1999 and miss him every day. *(Julie Crenshaw)*

Special moments like this one at Augusta in 1995 are especially meaningful with someone you love by your side. *(Frank Christian)*

In California, where we have a summer home, with Julie's family. Julie's parents, Warren and Sue Forrest, have *eight granddaughters!* (Maymie Molina)

I'm a late father, but Julie and the girls keep me young.
(from left) Katherine, Anna Riley, and Claire. *(Sue Forrest)*

I never stopped learning from Harvey. *(The Crenshaw Family Archives)*

For two years I heard it even more frequently.

Lanny Wadkins, who captained the 1995 team, told me that someday I might be captain but he never dwelled on it. Then, not long after Tom's team had lost at Valderrama, Jim Awtrey called. Awtrey, CEO of the PGA of America, needed to visit with me and was going to be in Fort Worth talking to the Colonial people about their Ryder Cup bid. He asked me to fly up and meet him at his hotel near DFW airport.

I knew what the subject would be—I would have had to be pretty naïve otherwise—but I certainly didn't know the process. I figured they would talk to four or five people, then make their choice.

But Jim started in right away, describing what the PGA does, what its legacy has been, and the role of PGA club professionals. The latter is an area close to my heart because of Harvey, and a lot of people from my era feel the same way. I told Jim that club pros were part of the fabric of the American golfer. They work hard and devote their lives to teaching and helping members to expand the game.

In Harvey's day a pro had to wear every hat. And, to an extent, they still do. Harvey and men like Claude Harmon gave lessons, sold green fees, and were the starters, the merchandisers, and the club repairmen. They did everything.

I was floored when Jim offered me the job on the spot. It was such a great honor, I jumped at it. I immediately thought of all the people I had grown up around, the people I had met in the game and the captains.

And, yes, I thought about Brookline. The Country Club again. I couldn't believe it. I was going back to Boston.

My first call was to Julie. The next to Curtis.

I had every reason in the world to believe they would pick Curtis to captain that team in Brookline. He'd won the first of his two consecutive U.S. Open titles there in 1988 and it seemed natural. Everyone seemed to think Curtis would be the pick, and I would have been fine with that.

I stammered a bit. "I wanted to call you because I've just been extended the Ryder Cup captaincy," I said. "I guess they picked me because I am older. But I wanted to call you and tell you because I know what The Country Club means to you."

He appreciated the call. "They can't pick us both," he said. "Maybe someday I'll be captain."

He was right, of course. He'll follow me as captain of the 2001 team in September 2002 at The Belfry. And, yes, he's been picking my brain.

Although I was sorry to see the 2001 Ryder Cup postponed, it was necessary. In light of the unspeakable terrorist acts in America on September 11, 2001, there was no other choice. Undoubtedly, there will be a different mood when the matches are finally played.

We kept my captaincy quiet until it was announced at the PGA's annual meeting and I was off and running. I did stop for a few minutes to think about how being captain might affect my game, but the fact was I wasn't really competitive at that point, at least as far as winning tournaments goes. The captain's job came at a good time in my life—as it has with many others—because I was in the process of winding down a little more. Tom Kite on the other hand was playing so well he almost played himself onto his own team. You still have to care so much about your game to do that, and I didn't.

I had already tested out the broadcast booth and, well, it wasn't for me. I lasted all of ten events.

Lance Barrow and Frank Chirkinian at CBS asked me to give it a try. I'd known them forever, and when they hired me as a color analyst I thought it was worth a shot. A lot of people saw that as a natural place for me because of my love of history and I enjoyed it. Well, a little bit.

Jackie Burke always says, "Once you climb up those stairs and into that TV tower, you're history. You can kiss your golf career goodbye." I thought about that, but was playing so badly Jackie's words seemed more like a relief than a caution. As it turned out it didn't matter.

I'm simply not quick enough for TV. It takes a Texan a full ten seconds to say hello. So you can only imagine. I'm still talking and they're ready to cut to another shot. I've gotten out one sentence and it's time for a commercial. I need time to tell a story, but more often than not in TV, you don't have time to tell a story.

I was in their way. They didn't have a place for me at that time. You've got to stick me in a box and give me a time and put the thing on tape. That's the only way I'll be any good at all.

Despite my frustrations, Scotty had gone to them just before the 1997 PGA Championship at Winged Foot to talk about extending my contract and finding a place for me. I even talked to Lance, the coordinating producer, that week, telling him I didn't think I was cut out for this. We left it at that—until that Sunday.

During that rain-delayed final round, I was in the tower at eighteen telling a story about Jackie Pung. In 1959 she had lost a tournament to Betsy Rawls at Winged Foot because she signed an incorrect scorecard. The members felt so bad for her they took up a collection to give her the equivalent of the first-place check. I thought it was a great story; something I could really contribute.

I had just started the story when I heard producer David Winner's voice in my ear. "You've got to throw it back to fifteen."

I love the guy. I love Lance. I love them all, but that was it. I took off my headset and walked out. Jim Nantz stopped me and said, "You have to finish the story." I told him no, I'm going down to see Davis. He's about to win this thing. And I just walked out. I never went back.

I viewed the captain's job as a fitting end to my career on the regular tour. There's no way you can succeed out there nowadays unless you have 100 percent total concentration on your golf game. Your mind can't be on anything else. I did that for twenty years and couldn't keep doing it. Jack and Arnold are exceptions. I have no idea how they played the kind of golf they did with all the things they had going on in their lives. They're almost superhumans. But today I see so much talent out there and so many young accomplished players. You've got to eat, sleep, and breathe it, and I wasn't.

Only a handful of guys have been competitive until their late forties, including Raymond, Jack, both Toms, and Hale Irwin. You have to admire the fabulous focus they had.

I was a late father and wanted to spend more time with my kids. And, I was concentrating more on Coore-Crenshaw. The captaincy allowed me to do both.

It wasn't long until I was immersed in Ryder Cup details. My chance was here and Julie was right there to share it—and the work. She thrust herself into it, organizing, ordering, planning, and designing.

And I picked up the phone and called Bruce Lietzke and Bill Rogers.

The job demands two assistants now and they were perfect. They are two of my closest friends—even if they did play at Houston—were Ryder Cup teammates of mine on that awesome 1981 team that won at Walton Heath, and they knew The Country Club. Bruce had played at that USGA Junior with me in 1968, and Bill had played in the Walker Cup matches I had passed up in 1973.

They knew me. They knew they were going to have to hold me together and that I was going to lean on them. I trusted their instincts implicitly; they would be my extra sets of eyes and ears. When they said yes, I couldn't have felt more blessed.

Everyone envies Bruce. He's so talented, he's competitive teeing it up just a dozen times a year. He's so mature and has never once wavered in his philosophy or approach to the game. He's confident, decisive, and puts things into perspective. For instance, if we were playing in Florida on a windy day with a thirty-mile-an-hour breeze, he wouldn't change his swing—he would just use two more clubs and rely on his beautiful, drowsy timing and that reliable fade of his.

Bill had been away from the Tour for a while, but I knew his experience would be invaluable. He had one of the most fabulous years in 1981, winning the British Open at Royal St. George's, the Australian Open, the World Match Play, the Suntory in Japan, the World Series of Golf, and the Texas Open, where he beat me in a playoff. He was also second to David Graham in the U.S. Open that year. Buck's nickname in college was Panther because he was always in motion—seemingly restless—the perfect complement to Bruce and me.

That spring before the matches we took a little fishing trip—just the three of us—to spend time thinking about what was ahead of us. We were in the middle of the lake when Julie called to tell us that Mark James had insisted the assistant captains be made part of the official party. They never had been before and there was reluctance on my and the PGA of America's part, but, in retrospect, it was proper. For Leaky and Buck it was the next best thing to being on the team.

I had been fortunate enough to play on four Ryder Cup teams, beginning with that 1981 team, captained by Dave Marr. We won there and again in 1983, but I was also part of the 1987 and 1995 teams that lost at Muirfield and Oak Hill, respectively. And, believe me, the emotions were extreme—from the unparalleled, exhilarating high of victory to the absolute gut-wrenching disappointment of defeat. The Ryder Cup is always a roller-coaster ride of emotions. I just didn't know we'd take them to a new level at Brookline.

I was lucky enough to have Dave Marr as captain of my first Ryder Cup team, and he was just as special as the competition. Long before the Ryder Cup became the mega-event it is now, the players knew it was special. The legacy had been passed down from all the great players in our history, because every one of them had played. And many of them also captained. There is a tremendous sense of history, playing for one's country, being part of a team.

But as great as that '81 team was, I still think there was a perception gap. I'm not sure the matches were as highly valued in this country as they are now, but they meant just as much to the players, I assure you. But when we lost at Muirfield and again at The Belfry two years later, America realized what the cup means.

I knew that if I was the third captain in a row who lost, I could expect all kinds of barbs. It's part of the job, I know, but personally, it meant a lot to me to try to do the best job possible because seeing

Lanny and Tom lose hurt me deeply. I played for Lanny and it killed me when we let him down. And Tom? How could that not hurt?

Neither one did anything wrong, but still got blamed. In my situation . . . it was different. After two losses we were playing a course that is not anything like a straightforward American golf course. You have to play it with feel and imagination, and I was determined to play whomever was playing the best and whomever had the best feel for that course. That was what it was going to boil down to.

I thought then, and still do, that there is a point where Americans think if we lose, it's an upset. That's simply not true. It's like going into a football game. You have to know your competition, what they can do, and you have to know your team. I certainly knew that our players had to play their best. There was absolutely no way we were going to be able to throw any surprises at the Europeans—they've seen it all and in all different weather conditions. That's what makes them tough. They're used to scoring under bad conditions and on courses that are not as well kept as ours. It's almost natural golf; it's instinctive golf. Exactly what you have to play at The Country Club.

Our game over here is played mostly in the air. And it's amazing the difference it makes. I knew adaptability would be an important ingredient. But the biggest factor would be Brookline itself.

It was the perfect place for the Ryder Cup at this stage in history. It's an old Eastern layout with its hilly, smallish greens, and until you get there and see it and play it you don't quite feel it. It's very different and has an imaginative layout, so to be successful there you have to know it. That's why I arranged a practice round for the team in August. And, at the start of the year, I encouraged everyone who was in contention for the team, if they were in the area, period, to go play The Country Club.

You simply cannot be ready for the emotions that you pack into one week and the little things you have to react to. There's no way. They hit you hard. And fast.

We did what we could to be ready for that week. I still daydream about it. I think about what I went through as a captain; what we went through as a team. The emotions. The moments. They're the rewards of being on a Ryder Cup team; memories that last forever.

I knew going in that I was exhausted. So before I went to Boston, I called the Buick people and told them I was not going to play the Buick Challenge at Callaway Gardens the week following the Ryder Cup.

"I'm the biggest basket case," I said. "I can't walk. I can't move. And by the time this week is over, I'll be no help to you at all."

They understood.

I don't know that I did. It seemed that two years had gone by in a flash; that Boston couldn't get here quickly enough, yet it also seemed to be here a bit too soon.

I was overwhelmed. I was excited.

I hoped I was ready.

14.

BACK TO BROOKLINE

NOTABLE RYDER CUP RECORDS

Most appearances: 11, Nick Faldo

Most points won by a European: 25, Nick Faldo

Most points won by an American: 231/2, Billy Casper

Most wins as pair: 11, Seve Ballesteros and Jose Maria Olazabal

Biggest last-day comeback to win: 4 points, U.S.A., 1999

It was just the two of us—Julie and I holding hands in the back seat of the Town Car as our driver made the ninety-minute trip down from Maine. We were anxious, wondering how the week in front of us would unfold.

We couldn't believe it was here. We went over details, wondering what we'd missed. We went over lists of things to follow up on when we arrived. We wondered what we could do to make the team play its best. What should I say? Would the players be excited as we were?

The team would be arriving over the next twenty-four hours and we wanted everything to be perfect. We'd worked so hard.

We each took a deep breath as the car pulled up to the front door of the Four Seasons. Here we were. Here it was.

The last six weeks had been tumultuous; the last few days a slice of heaven.

We'd finally taken former President and Mrs. Bush up on an invitation for lobsters and golf at their home in Kennebunkport. They'd asked us several times since we attended a state dinner at the White House and this seemed the perfect time. I had played golf with the senior Bush several times at Barton Creek Country Club and we had talked on other occasions. It was an easy friendship, though much more formal than the one I have with his son, George W. Bush.

George W.—*President* Bush—and I met years ago through my friend Bill Munn. We saw each other occasionally when he and Laura were living in Dallas, and I went to some baseball games with him when he was managing partner of the Texas Rangers. We struck up a warm friendship. Julie and I had a fund-raiser for him at the house when he ran for governor of Texas and we attended the same church. He and Laura have always been frequent visitors to the house since moving to Austin—Scotty even coached their daughter Jenna in softball—and they made time during the campaign to relax and kick back with us on weekends. With the Secret Service in tow, of course.

George W. can hit the ball pretty well and would be a good player if he had more time. But his pace of play is like his dad's—he usually wants to stay in motion.

I have to say Kennebunkport is in a beautiful setting. And it was fun playing Cape Arundel. I rode with former President Bush but played with his nephew Craig Stapleton. The former President teamed with the head pro, Ken Raynor, and beat us, one-up. And, yes, we played very quickly.

There weren't many groups out, but we did play through a fund-raiser for Vermont senator Olympia Snowe. Oklahoma senator Don Nickles was there too and we stopped for a moment to meet them, then we were off and flying again. It was all very informal, very relaxing.

Former President Bush had taped a little clip for the video we planned to show later in the week, so there was no question he was behind us. But he reminded us just the same, saying they'd be coming to Brookline and didn't want to be in the way, but did want us to know they'd be pulling for us.

I got up early Sunday morning and was walking down the hall, and there was Barbara Bush in her PJs, sitting on the bed with her laptop. She looked up and said, "Hey Ben." She's so unpretentious, so gracious. It's no wonder the whole country just wants to hug her.

It was the perfect getaway from the details, the nerves, and the remnants of the turmoil that had greeted me at the PGA Championship the previous month.

Money. The issue has been brought up before—just never publicly. Call it pay-for-play, compensation, or a designated donation for members of the Ryder Cup team. The players had discussed it, but among themselves. Now, a little more than a month before the matches, they were talking to reporters and the headlines were everywhere.

Tom Kite had mentioned this might happen. He saw it bubbling on the horizon and gave me a heads-up. I wasn't caught off guard by the notion, but I was stunned that it was the hottest topic going. I came to Chicago with my mind on finalizing the team, making my wild card picks, and seeing how everyone was playing. I didn't want any other distractions. But I got them.

The press was all over the issue—who was for it, who was against it, and just what the stakes were, period. It got so heated early that week that I talked with several players individually, trying to sort things out. The PGA of America was concerned enough to call a special meeting with potential Ryder Cup team members to address the situation. Unfortunately nothing was settled at the meeting.

I was part of an era when payment for the Ryder Cup team wasn't ever discussed. You played for your country, period. But today's top players have difficult decisions to make with respect to where they play and where to concentrate their efforts, and I was certain this was a basis for their viewpoint. It was a painful time for all of us and both sides suffered, but at the meeting the PGA of America promised to address the issue immediately after the Ryder Cup, and they did. A few months later the PGA determined that the captain and each player could make $200,000 each in designated donations—$100,000 to the university of their choice and $100,000 to the charity of their choice.

The meeting with the PGA did quiet things down because it had been an ongoing problem since the British Open and had simmered. It kind of evaporated when we left Chicago, which was good for everyone. My concern was that the focus of my players was not on the matches. In retrospect, while it was uncomfortable at the time, it was certainly a good thing that it came up in Chicago—well before we got to Boston.

It's amazing. The Ryder Cup has been played since 1927 and nothing like this has ever come up. It has always been simply an issue of playing for your country—or now, countries. The original format had teams from the U.S. and Great Britain playing each other every two years. But in 1979 the Great Britain team was expanded to include all of Europe. Over the years, the size of the team has grown from an original nine players per team to the current twelve and the format has been tweaked several times. Today's format is twenty-eight matches— eight four-balls, eight foursomes, and twelve singles matches.

For a few days it seemed the compensation issue was bigger than the tournament, but by the weekend everyone was focused on Sergio Garcia battling Tiger down to the wire at Medinah. I was shut up in the players' dining room that final day, watching the telecast to see who was going to play their way onto—or off of—the team and contemplating my wild card choices. Lanny dropped by and so did quite a few players. I had lists of cellphone numbers tucked in my pocket—just in case I had to find someone jetting across the country.

I had always said one pick would be fairly obvious and one would keep me up at night. And that's what happened.

Coming into that week it was troublesome. So much depended on how certain people played. They could either play their way on or off the team, and how that unfolded would affect my two choices. Tom Lehman was an obvious pick. He'd been playing so well and was very determined. And, he commanded the respect of every player. He tied for thirty-fourth, but that didn't enter my thoughts at all.

Going into the final day both Bob Estes and Steve Pate had chances to make the team on points and bump Jeff Maggert out of tenth place. Bob needed to finish no worse than a two-way tie for fifth and was right there until he bogeyed two of the last three holes. Steve had to finish third to pick up enough points, but finished tied for eighth.

Had one of those two played their way on, I might have looked at my picks differently. As it was, I went into the week looking at those two as well as Lehman, Freddie Couples, Chris Perry, Lee Janzen, Steve Stricker, and Jeff Sluman, who's so consistent I knew he would play well in Brookline. Freddie told me he was playing well, and, as I've said before, even when he isn't playing well he's one of the best players in the game. But I was worried about him being able to play twice a day with his bad back, and he hadn't played that much.

Then, I realized that Steve had been playing the best golf of his life and he knew The Country Club. He had tied for third there behind Curtis in 1988. He was focused, feisty, and tough. The more I thought about him, the more I recalled how well he got along with everyone and how he would add a different dimension to the team. Sarcastic in his humor, he's always making fun of himself.

Some members of the press were surprised when I picked him. They thought Freddie was a lock. But I sounded out several former captains and they all thought Steve was a great pick.

The two toughest things a captain has to do is make calls to the players he doesn't pick and tell players during the matches they have to sit down. I didn't like doing either. It was really tough.

After I called Pate and Lehman, my team was set—Tiger Woods, David Duval, Justin Leonard, Davis Love III, Jim Furyk, Hal Sutton,

Jeff Maggert, Mark O'Meara, Phil Mickelson, Payne Stewart, Pate, and Lehman. The European team consisted of Lee Westwood, Darren Clarke, Jesper Parnevik, Sergio Garcia, Jose Maria Olazabal, Colin Montgomerie, Jean Van de Velde, Miguel Angel Jimenez, Jarmo Sandelin, Paul Lawrie, Padraig Harrington, and Andrew Coltart. Coming out of Chicago the one thing I was worried about was our focus. The differences of opinion had derailed us a bit and I felt we were way behind in focus compared to the Europeans. That's one reason I encouraged everyone to come to the practice round we scheduled the Monday after the World Series of Golf. Only Tiger, Mark, Tom, and Davis missed the trip—the first three because of previous commitments; Davis because of his ailing back—but even then, the focus was on the team and the matches, and that's obviously what I wanted.

The trip to Brookline was great. It was the first chance to be together as a team and the first opportunity a lot of players had to meet Buck. He had been away from the Tour for nearly a decade, working as director of golf at San Antonio Country Club, but he had kept up with players and jumped right in as though he'd barely been gone.

We wanted the players to enjoy the day and learn the course, but we also had to have fun and some of it came at Payne's expense. He and Pater—that's what I call Steve—had been out drinking with some of the caddies the night before and Scotty was quickly dispatched to find him a cheeseburger to help cure the hangover. Payne, of course, took it in stride and dished out as much grief as he took.

I absolutely listened to whatever the players said about pairings, and that practice round created one of our best partnerships—Hal and Jeff. They enjoyed playing together that day, saw a chemistry, and both told me they wanted to be paired. I came away knowing that was one pairing that wouldn't change—on the first day, at least.

The more I got with people, the better. All my other pairings were just thoughts, and I got input from everyone including my caddie, Linn Strickler, and Tom Watson's caddie Bruce Edwards, who were also part of my captain's squad. Sometimes it was just "I want to tell you something I'm thinking," sometimes it was more concrete. We took it all in.

When you finally get there and the gravity of the week hits you like a thud—it's game time. It's your hopes and your fears. The apprehension. We knew that and planned for it.

Our first team dinner was so relaxed. We told the guys to throw on T-shirts and jeans and we headed to the Union Oyster House down by the Back Bay. It's the oldest restaurant in the United States and I thought it would be a really neat way to say, "We're in Boston."

We realized that quickly. When the bus pulled up to the restaurant, hundreds of people were there cheering, clapping, and waving flags. I don't know how they knew we would be there, but they did. And it was fun to watch the guys' faces. It was incredible. There's a big picture window that frames the front of the restaurant where we started out eating shucked oysters and having a beer, and people kept peeping in. We had a nice dinner—the PGA of America gave us our Ryder Cup rings and Julie even had Ryder Cup lobster bibs made for everyone— and, to our surprise, people were still cheering outside when we left.

And it didn't stop there. On the way to practice one day, Buck, Scotty, and I left for the course a little after 6 A.M. We wanted to get out there and have everything in place for the practice round. We got to the light where you turn off to go to the club and it was really congested. Just then, a guy in an old, red Volvo looked over and said, "Mr. Crenshaw, go get 'em." Then he gets out of his car—the light has turned green—and comes over to get an autograph. I was so focused I didn't realize we were holding up traffic until I heard all the horns honking and people cussin' and carrying on.

Our team room at the hotel, I must say, was the place to be that week. Payne came to us early that year with a suggestion.

"I have a way to help the team," he said with that impish grin of his. "It's a Ping-Pong table."

Julie and I looked at each other, then at him. "Trust me. It's a way to blow off steam, have fun, and be together."

And, knowing Payne, a way for him to get in a little trash talk.

We also had a big-screen TV and a room with a Play Station. Julie had decorated the halls with posters of American champions like Lance Armstrong and vintage photographs of American Ryder Cup teams.

During the week it seemed that everyone from Prince Andrew to Stephen Tyler to the Backstreet Boys dropped by.

Julie did an incredible job of organizing things. The players' clothes were all in their rooms and we had a tailor on call just in case—and believe me, we needed him.

Badgley Mischka had designed the women's gowns for the gala and Oxxford did the men's tuxedos. A few pants had to be hemmed and Tiger's jacket wasn't ready. He was working out and was the last one to be measured and he came up with sleeve problems that night. He was cool about going jacketless. Julie and Sue Martin from the PGA had the alterations done and Tiger's jacket was delivered while the dinner was in progress. He looked great, and Julie was excited to see him wearing that same tux months later at the ESPY awards.

To make everything perfect, Julie also ordered gifts for everyone—for every night—and our secretary Kimberly Johnson was assigned to deliver them. She started off with yellow roses and cookie bouquets—complete with a Ryder Cup golf bag cookie with the player's name on it—and kept things coming. A yellow Herend squirrel, signifying The Country Club. A silver Ryder Cup dish. A leather Ryder Cup desk set. An etched bottle of Opus I wine. A cigar box. A tiny Limoges Ryder Cup trophy.

The wives had been calling her the "gift fairy" all week, then pulled a joke on her when it was time to present her with their gift. Instead of the traditional silver box, they gave her a really ugly brooch. She didn't know what to say—until Ashley Sutton, the ringleader, admitted it was a joke.

As for the rings? The team was so proud of them, although we've already had to replace one. Tom lost his digging in the dirt somewhere playing with his son Thomas.

The practice rounds went well and only two players were upset with themselves. Steve wasn't happy with his driving and Mark came in not playing as well as he would have liked. Wednesday afternoon he went out by himself for a nine-hole spin and I caught up with him at the twelfth hole to visit for a few minutes.

"I've been practicing all summer," he said. "It's frustrating not to see it come together. I'm trying so hard."

I shook my head. "God bless, Mark. After the year you had last year, winning two majors and having a great season, it's understandable. Just do the best you can. That's what everyone's going to do."

Everyone else seemed ready to go.

Scotty had found some magnetic boards to use as we worked on the pairings. And did they ever get a workout. Each captain is responsible for submitting his slate of players for each session at a time agreed to by the captains and both the PGA of America and the European PGA Tour. What makes this difficult is one captain has no idea who the other will pair together or in what order. Each captain pairs his players and sets a lineup which is then matched against the other team.

All matches are decided by match play rules—holes are won, lost, or tied—as opposed to medal play, which is decided by individual stroke totals. One point is awarded to a team for each match won, but if a match is tied after 18 holes, each team receives one-half of a point. In order win the Ryder Cup, a team must accumulate 14½ points. But in case of a 14–14 tie, the team that last won the Ryder Cup retains the trophy.

Mark James knew who his horses were and he wasn't going to deviate from his pairings. I think we had more combinations, more interchangeable parts. We had pretty much settled on our first-day pairings on Wednesday night. Scotty, Buck, Bruce, and I slipped out of the team room, went down to my room, and brainstormed. Some pairings were simple; others weren't. But when we went to bed that night I felt pretty good about our choices.

Those first pairings had to be turned in just before the opening ceremonies, so we got together again to give it one last look. I had a gut feeling and changed one thing—I put Payne into the lineup for Justin, pairing him with Davis. I knew I was pairing Justin and Davis, two really close friends, in the afternoon.

That done, we took the pairings over and got them in with plenty of time to spare. It was the only time. We did push it every other time. I can still hear Kerry Haigh of the PGA telling us to hurry up. Time was up. It was never easy to make the lineups, but I knew that whatever happened, the team was behind me.

Just before the opening ceremonies I walked through the locker room and Hal was sitting in front of his locker. He stopped me.

"Ben, I know you're going to do what you want to do," he said. "You've got an idea of where you want to go and who you're going to pair. But the one thing the USA has been guilty of in the past is not playing to win.

"If I could make one suggestion to you, this is it—if my place is on the bench, that's where I want to be. And I think that's the way everyone feels."

That told me we were ready. We were ready to win.

15.

I BELIEVE IN FATE

WHERE FATE LENT A HAND

Francis Ouimet winning the 1913 U.S. Open at The Country Club
Jack Nicklaus winning the 1986 Masters
Bobby Jones winning the 1930 British Amateur at St. Andrews
Ken Venturi winning the 1964 U.S. Open at Congressional
Davis Love winning the 1997 PGA at Winged Foot
1995 Masters
U.S. winning the 1999 Ryder Cup

It was late Friday afternoon by the time we all gathered back together in the locker room and, yes, we were frustrated. No one kicked a trash can. No one slammed a locker. A few expletives that weren't deleted flew around the room, but it was understandable.

Our team was so strong. On paper we had the edge. We were playing at home. We had put some awesome combinations onto the course. And we were down 6–2?

I couldn't believe it. We couldn't believe it. Those pairings we'd worked so hard on weren't jelling. It wasn't the start we were hoping for.

As a captain that's the worst feeling—a feeling of futility. You know your players. You can see they're playing well. You know they're ready. And, suddenly, you come up against one of those wild days. A putt here, a shot there and we're off and running. Instead, anything that could happen did—for the Europeans.

The good news? We've all had days like that and we've all survived them. And that's what mattered.

Phil was upset about his putting. He'd missed two great chances in the final three holes and he and Jim had lost 1-up in the afternoon to Sergio and Jesper. That morning he and David, who wasn't driving the way he wanted, had lost the first match of the matches 3-and-2 to Paul Lawrie and Colin. David and Tiger—how can you beat that combination?—had lost to Darren Clarke and Lee Westwood 1-up in the afternoon. David and Tiger both felt they had left shots on the course.

Our only points had come from Hal and Jeff's 3-and-2 win over Clarke and Westwood in the morning and two halves—one by Payne and Davis in the morning; a second from Davis and Justin in the afternoon.

Everyone was shaking their head—even the players who felt good about their games and their day.

Frustrating and excruciating. Those were the terms I had used with reporters that night. It was excruciating for me all day—and chaotic. I'm trying to decide where I need to be, where my assistants are, and what kinds of decisions need to be made for the next set of pairings. And, I'm watching my team play so well, but come up *just this* short.

We were all frustrated, but the situation wasn't as dire as the reporters wanted to make it sound. The Europeans had played very well, and being down by four points was a slight strain—the kind you have when the leader of a Tour event opens with a 64 and you shoot the worst score you could have—a 71 or 72. At that point you know you can make up ground. Seven or eight shots with three rounds to go is infinitesimally small. The guys knew that being down by four points here was the same thing. It was too early to be feeling disconsolate.

In the locker room I told the guys tomorrow would be better; that four points weren't many with twenty matches left—eight more pairings on Saturday and twelve singles on Sunday. And Hal told a story about what he'd learned at his first Ryder Cup back in 1985.

"We can't play to keep something bad from happening," he said. "We have to play to make something good happen."

He was so right. The last thing we needed was to start playing defensively. I knew this team too well. I knew we wouldn't. This team was filled with veterans who weren't going to dwell on a day like Friday. They were tired—especially the guys who had played two matches—and everyone opted for an easy night in the team room. A little takeout from everyone's favorite—P. F. Chang's, just around the corner. A little Ping-Pong. A little hanging out. An early night.

I can't tell you how much respect I have for Hal. What he did that week—the things he said, the way he played, how he went about everything—was so impressive. He might be the straightest shooter I have ever seen. He'll tell you exactly what's on his mind and that's what we needed to hear. He was the backbone of that team—in actions, deeds, and words.

Hal did as much to lift our spirits, maybe more, than anybody else on the team. He laid out his barest heart to us and said, "This is what it's going to take to get it done." And he was right on target.

He's been through so much in his career—and life—and now he's so peaceful. There are no more storms in Hal Sutton. The storms are over. He has a totally different countenance around him. He lifts everyone. And he lifted us that night.

"We're just going to have to reach down inside and pull something out," he said. "We're all going to have to play well. One person can't play well and the other not. We're all going to have to reach down. We're all good players. We can do that."

We had to.

That first day had been a blur.

David and Phil were our first group out against Colin and Lawrie and, after halving the first five holes, we took the lead at the sixth with Phil's flop shot two feet from the hole. It was our only lead of that match. Lawrie tied it back up on the next hole, they went ahead on the eighth, and we tied it again on the ninth. Then Europe took off.

We three-putted the tenth when Phil missed a two and a half footer and before we knew it, Europe was 3-up and on the way to a 3-and-2 win. Then Tiger and Tom lost 2-and-1 to Sergio and Jesper and . . . well, so much for the fast start we had hoped for.

Tom had holed a thirty-foot chip on the first hole, but this match was so even. The Europeans took the lead for good at the twelfth when we three-putted from forty-five feet, and Jesper made two key putts down the stretch—a ten-foot par save at fourteen and an eight-footer at the seventeenth, the latter coming just after Tom missed from ten feet. Tom, who's always so solid, missed a couple on the last four holes.

We did finally get a half point in the third match when Davis and Payne halved their match with Miguel Angel Jimenez and Padraig Harrington. We were 2-up after four holes, but three-putted for bogey—from twelve feet—at the fifth. The Europeans did the same thing, but we knew we had missed a chance to take them out of the match quickly, or at least give them something to think about.

It seemed to be a recurring theme for us all day.

Davis squared the match with a big putt at the seventeenth to take the match to eighteen where we halved, then Hal and Jeff came up big. They actually trailed by two after four holes, but Hal made three birdies in a row to give them a 1-up lead. They closed out the match with birdies at fourteen and sixteen. I can't tell you how important that win was. It gave us a point, a strong pairing, and, we hoped, a little momentum going into the afternoon.

I thought about keeping my pairings together, but it was evident we needed a change. I did keep Hal and Jeff together, but I shuffled the rest, pairing Davis with Justin, Furyk with Phil, and Tiger with Duval for the afternoon four-ball—actually best-ball—matches.

One of the toughest pairings was anyone with Tiger. Probably anybody in the world who's paired with Tiger, they're trying to help him as much as possible. You kind of scratch your head and say, "What do I do to help this guy?" You want to get a player in there who plays well enough to free him up as well.

I could see that first day he was feeling a little pressure—we all were—and that afternoon was when I started thinking about pairing him with Pater on Saturday. In fact, someone even mentioned it. Tiger had played with Pater's brother John in California, and Pater has that way of keeping everyone loose. The more I thought about it the better it sounded.

But back to Friday. We got our afternoon pairings in, watched the morning matches finish up, then took a break—if you could call it that. The only thing you can do between the morning and afternoon sessions is grab a sandwich and run. We did that and I was back, darting from match to match with Scotty driving and me jumping out from time to time to chat.

We really thought we could turn it around, but we took it on the chin and fell further behind. Out of four possible points in the afternoon, we won one-half of a point, that coming when Davis and Justin halved with Paul and Colin in the first afternoon match.

On the eighteenth hole Davis had a huge twenty-footer for birdie to halve the match. I was standing on the back of the green and Davis looked at me and asked, "What does this putt do?"

Not that he really needed the help, but I went out and took a look. During matches, your partner, your caddie, or the captain are the only people who can advise you and, during singles, only the captain or your caddie. I was glad to help—in fact, that's the only putt I read all week. I sized it up and told him it broke about two feet outside the left lip.

"I never would have played it that far," he said.

But he did, it broke, and went right into the middle of the cup. He looked at me, and Justin ran over and started slapping him on the back—and back end. Colin just missed a downhill fifteen-footer that would have won the match. That one-half point was all we would get.

In the second match we shot a better-ball 62—that's ten-under—and Phil and Jim lost to Sergio and Jesper, who were having a great day, 1-up. That's what happens in match play. One key shot is all you need sometimes, and Jesper got it, holing a 9-iron from 140 yards out at the eighth hole. He also made enough seriously tough putts to last a lifetime.

Hal and Maggert never got untracked and lost to Jose Maria and Jimenez 2-and-1, then Tiger and Duval lost 1-up. That last match lasted—if you can believe it—five and a half hours. I'm sorry, but that's way too long. Something was up and I made a mental note to figure out what. I wouldn't like what I would discover.

That last one really hurt. Clarke and Westwood are arguably two of Europe's top players, yet our guys are the top two players in the world. We needed that point and everyone knew it. That match drew a crowd, including Michael Jordan and former President Bush and his wife Barbara.

But Tiger and Duval led for just one hole—when Tiger chipped in from fifteen yards for a birdie at the tenth. Clarke found his putting touch at the right time and made a ten-foot birdie at number seventeen for a birdie that gave Europe its 1-up lead. Westwood chipped close enough to the hole at eighteen that we conceded his par putt to end the match at dusk—with barely enough light to see the ball on the green.

Down 6–2? Only about three dozen cameras and several hundred reporters wanted to know what the heck was wrong.

By the time I faced them I had already met with the team and turned in my lineup for Saturday morning. Let me tell you, we'd get in a room—both Bruces, Buck, Scotty, Linn, and I—and we'd start talking. We had about as much fun as we possibly could doing it, but it was like someone wringing you out like a towel. We had decided to keep Hal and Maggert together, pair Tiger and Pater, Furyk and Mark, and put Payne and Justin together. Payne, Justin, and Davis were just so tough. All three of them matched well and it was hard sitting someone down, but I let Davis rest along with Duval, Phil, and Tom.

At the press room the questions kept coming and I had the same answers. I had seen a load of putts just graze the edges of holes and stay out. And, like the Tiger-Duval pairing, there was a very fine line between straining for a result and just allowing yourself to let things happen. It was only the first day, but the reporters were ready to bury us.

Neither Mark nor Steve played Friday, but they kept loose by playing a few holes behind the day's final match. Both of them were disappointed—"I'd be lying if I said I wasn't disappointed," Mark told reporters—but understood.

Before he left for the hotel, Tom summed things up. "We didn't take advantage of our chances. That won't go on forever."

When I put together our game plan for the actual matches, I knew I wanted one of my assistants with every match. A captain simply can't be everywhere, but with Buck, Leaky, Bruce, and Linn all on walkie-talkies and in carts, I knew we'd have a good set of eyes on everyone and they'd keep me informed. I wanted to know anything they noticed, if a player was playing well or having trouble.

Bruce Edwards and Linn were so important. I needed a couple of guys I could rely on to take care of little things—a glove, towel, an umbrella, whatever. I also wanted to draw on their past experience and expertise. Both are about the same age and each has seen twenty-five-years-plus of tournament golf. Any little thing they said carried weight because they got hunches, too. A caddie can read a player more quickly sometimes than another player. They did all that and anything more we asked.

On top of everything else going on, showers halted play Saturday morning for a short time. Everyone was scrambling for their rain-suit and we looked everywhere for Tiger's—his locker, caddie Steve Williams' locker—but couldn't find it. It was back in his room. So Leaky gave him his jacket. But for a while there the only thing you could hear on the walkie-talkies was us searching high and low.

Saturday was going to be pivotal. We needed to get started with a bang, so we sent Hal and Maggert out first against Colin and Lawrie. It took five hours and a twenty-minute lightning delay, but we won it, 1-up. Colin was getting heckled by a few fans but played well, and the match went into seventeen all square. That's when Maggert got his twenty-five-footer to plop into the hole to give us a lead and, when putts were conceded by both sides at the eighteenth, we had another point.

That match showed us how close the two teams were. Every time we challenged, they responded. And despite winning four of the day's eight matches, we didn't make up any ground, ending the day down 10–6.

Mark and Furyk led their match through five holes but couldn't hold off Clarke and Westwood, who won 3-and-2. They squared the match at the sixth, then Westwood put them up for good at the ninth.

Finally we found an ideal partner for Tiger in Pater. Steve can flat-out play, he's a cold-blooded putter, and he'd run through a wall for you. His sense of humor relaxed Tiger and they picked up another point with a 1-up win over Jimenez and Harrington.

Tiger and Pater won the first three holes, but nine holes and a rain delay later it was all square. Tiger said afterward that he and Steve knew coming down the stretch that their match was a point we had to have, and they came through. The key was fourteen, where Tiger boomed one off the tee, Pater's approach landed thirty feet from the pin, and Tiger rolled in the eagle for a 1-up lead.

Justin and Payne tried to slow down Sergio and Jesper—the hottest team of the matches at that point—but they couldn't. Sergio and Jesper moved to 3–0 with a 3-and-2 win that was decided early when our guys had five bogeys and the Europeans had five birdies in the first eleven holes.

Because of the rain delay, matches were still on the course when I had to turn in the afternoon pairings, but I knew one thing—I was going to break up Hal and Jeff. Both of them had come to me and asked for it. They knew they were a good team in alternate shot, but Jeff was missing a few shots. Hal said it with Maggert standing right there. Both of them were getting tired, but Hal wanted to go back out.

I wasn't going to break up Tiger and Pater, I wanted Davis and Duval to play together, and Tom and Phil. So who was going out with Hal?

I was on the walkie-talkie with Leaky and Buck. Buck was with Jim and Mark, who needed to know if they were warming up or sitting out. Leaky was with Payne and Justin, and Justin came over and said, "Tell Ben I want to go back out."

When a player says that I know he's ready, so I paired him with Hal. I had a hunch, deep down, that he was going to make a putt. I was right. Just had the wrong day.

The press questioned that move. So did NBC's Johnny Miller, who said during the telecast, "My hunch is that Justin should go home and watch on television." The guys heard about that Saturday night and, well, let's just say it was one more thing to motivate us. Like we didn't have enough already.

This was one day I really pushed the pairings deadline. I'm on the walkie-talkie and Kerry Haigh is standing not far away saying, "Give me the pairings." I got them done, but they were right at the bell—and only then because they were a bit lenient due to the rain delay.

Another quick lunch and we were ready for the four-balls. Duval had been bothered by his driving, but he felt better Saturday afternoon.

We were standing on the clubhouse porch when I told him, "Take those big shoulders of yours and remember to get that club all the way back to the end of your backswing. And give it hell."

He did.

Phil changed putters overnight, found his touch Saturday morning, and he and Tom gave us a 2-and-1 victory over Clarke and Westwood in the first afternoon match. The shot of the match was Phil's wedge from one hundred yards at the tenth that finished in tap-in range to give us a 3-up lead.

But, darn it, that was the only full point we got in the afternoon. Davis and Duval halved their match with Sergio and Jesper, and Justin and Hal halved their match against Jimenez and Olazabal. Whatever my reasoning was, Tiger and Pate played well in the four-ball but still lost, 2-and-1, to Colin and Lawrie. Colin is a great player and he proved it again with six birdies in that match, the last one a fifteen-footer at the fifteenth that gave them a 1-up lead. Tiger had his share of chances, too. He just couldn't make the putts.

Sergio and Jesper were unbelievable. Sergio sank a six-footer at the eighteenth to halve the match, then jumped into Jesper's arms. We should have expected that. I mean, he even gave Julie a kiss during the match.

I only wished I felt as energetic. Hal and Justin spent most of their match trying to pull even. They were 1-down at the par-three sixteenth when Sutton's 6-iron stopped about an inch to the right of the hole for a birdie that would even the match. And Justin had a chance to maybe win it at the seventeenth after Jimenez missed a twelve-footer for birdie. But Justin left a fifteen-footer just short.

That hole, it turned out, owed him one.

At the end of the day we were still down by four and the press was circling. No team in Ryder Cup history had ever come from four down to win. This wasn't just a 10–6 European lead, it was about to be a European knockout.

Or was it? There were still twelve matches left. We knew we could do it. It didn't matter what the press was saying.

"It's not that high of a hill," Hal said. "I think we've got twelve great players on this team. We've shown a lot of fight this week and I think we can show some more."

When I looked at their eyes those first two days, I could see how much they were hurting. Their sense of pain was what all of us had felt when we played for Lanny at Oak Hill and lost. It's what the team was feeling in Spain with Tom. You feel double pain, triple pain, because you can more easily accept a mistake when you make one and you're out there yourself. But gosh, you want to do your best for your team, and when you don't, you just feel awful.

At the same time, they knew this wasn't over. We all sat around in the locker room as I made out the singles lineup. The players refused to put their heads down and so did I. After sending in the lineup, I sent the players back to the hotel and went to the press tent.

I had a feeling that Hal was right.

Mark James was finished with his press conference and I took the hot seat. I was dog-tired and, to be honest, I was asked a lot of inane questions, a lot of the same questions. My mind was stale and I'm sure I looked very frazzled. I just wanted to get out of there, get back to the hotel, and rest.

I'd had no chance to regroup and collect my thoughts. My brain was on overload. And it showed.

My opening comment was something like, "I know we've reached a long and exciting day." What I meant to say was the end of a long and exciting day. But . . . I rolled on from there.

In my mind we had more than a chance. I had seen our team do good things out there. So had some of the former captains. Raymond turned to me at one point in the afternoon and said, "I feel something in the trees."

I knew we would need the biggest last-day comeback in history, and there were twelve points out there. We needed eight and a half. I was thinking like a captain; like a player. We were great singles players and I saw no reason to be anything but positive . . . even if I was one of the few in that room who believed it.

I was proud of my guys and I said it. Then a reporter asked me—considering that two points was the largest deficit any team had ever overcome—to use one word to describe our deficit.

"Everybody is collectively playing well," I said. Well, not only was that four words, it didn't answer the question. By then my train of thought was on another question and I was struggling. I found out later that Bruce and Scotty were watching the press conference on television in the locker room. "He's rambling," Bruce said. "We've got to get him out of there."

I got myself out instead. The press wanted me to say, in effect, that we didn't have a chance, and I wasn't going to say something I didn't believe. And, I wasn't going to say anything that left a question in anyone's mind. I didn't want the players to hear that.

I was so tired that when someone asked why the Europeans had mastered the four-balls and foursomes in recent years and the Americans hadn't, I didn't know what to say. I never have. They just do it better.

What I wanted to say was, they're comfortable playing damned slow. Like those five-and-a-half-hour rounds.

Then, twice in a row, the same question from two different reporters. The same 4-down question that had already been asked. I snapped. I really felt in my heart that the matches were much closer than what the margins showed, and I thought everyone was putting way too much importance on the margins. And, I knew that fate or something was going to take care of us. It happens every time on that golf course.

As all that was running through my head, something jolted me back into reality.

I looked straight at the crowd and pointed my finger at them.

"I'm going to leave you all with one thought, and I'm going to leave. I'm a big believer in fate. I have a good feeling about this. That's all I am going to tell you."

With that, I got up out of my chair, walked off the stage, and was out the door.

16.

TAKING DEAD AIM

BIGGEST GOLF UPSETS

Billy Casper overtakes Arnold Palmer to win 1966 U.S. Open at Olympic
Jack Fleck defeats Ben Hogan to win 1955 U.S. Open at Olympic
Francis Ouimet defeats Harry Vardon and Ted Ray to win 1913 U.S. Open
Sam Snead never wins a U.S. Open
Arnold Palmer and Tom Watson never win a PGA Championship
Europeans win their first Ryder Cup on U.S. soil in 1987 at Muirfield Village

Little did I know, but a number of my players were gathered around the television in the team room when I left the press with that thought. They cheered. Reporters shook their heads—they thought I was certifiable.

A number of them told several Texas reporters that I had "lost it." How in the world could I be talking about fate with my team down by four points? They didn't understand. And I don't know that I expected them to.

I wish I could say that I had planned the whole thing, rehearsed it for dramatic effect, and then used my words as a motivational tool. But I can't. It just busted out.

Scotty even assumed I'd saved that up. All I can say is, I knew I wasn't going anywhere or adding anything useful by answering the questions. I wasn't making any sense and I was just trying not to say anything wrong. Then this came out of my mouth.

We had a great singles lineup and I felt we were on the verge of something big. I didn't know what it was at the time; I really didn't. But I knew this match was going to be close. I had the feeling Brookline was going to take care of us because it's always been good to Americans. And I did believe in fate. How could I not after Harvey guided me to that second Masters? I could give you a million other examples of things you don't have control over but have a feeling will happen—like Davis winning the PGA at Winged Foot, playing the way he did and finishing it framed in that rainbow on eighteen.

As Bobby Jones' biographer O. B. Keeler said, some men call it fate. I believe that. That's why I said it.

I walked into the team room and Davis jumped up. "Way to go!" Their mouths had dropped when I closed out my press conference. They couldn't believe that I said exactly what they were thinking.

A few minutes later Julius Mason walked in with the day's quote sheets and transcripts. One quote on the sheet jumped out—one from Colin:

"You know we've won, don't you. It's silent. Great, and that's the best thing we can do—silence the crowd by outplaying them."

The team was already mad about what Johnny Miller said. Now this. I can tell you it didn't go over very well. And, as more than one player put it—"Yeah, it's over all right. But they've got the wrong team."

What a way to start off the night. Everyone was sitting on the floor in jeans and T-shirts, finishing up the last bit of food from P. F. Chang's. The room was buzzing.

That set the tone and we followed it with a thirty-minute video that Mickey Holden put together for us. I actually had to talk a little longer than I planned because at the last minute Mickey decided to splice in some highlights from Saturday's round.

We saw many terrific shots out there that afternoon, and when I was going around the course with Tom Kite, Raymond, and Lanny, they saw them too. The cheers were reverberating and our players heard them. We knew the difference between an American cheer and one for Europe, and we were gaining confidence, coming together.

Mickey's video reinforced everything. It started with great Ryder Cup moments laid over Frank Sinatra's "Here's To The Winners" and was a masterful mix of motivation, inspiration, and just plain fun. He'd included George C. Scott's "kick 'em in the ass" speech from *Patton* and scenes from *Caddyshack* and *Animal House*—like John Belushi's famous "Nothing's over 'til we say it's over"—and the *Blues Brothers*. Encouraging words came from former President Bush, Jay Leno, the Dallas Cowboy cheerleaders, Pamela Anderson, Dan Marino, members of the band REM, Sammy Sosa, and Kordell Stewart. We also saw clips of great moments in every player's career and a couple of memos to Europe:

> *The party is over.*
> *The Cup stays here.*

Just as the video ended, then-Texas governor George W. Bush, who had been watching the matches with his mother and father, walked in to say good luck. We had talked about this a few weeks before. I thought we might be in a tough situation, so I asked him to drop by and read Col. William B. Travis' letter from the Alamo. "You don't have to stay but a couple of minutes," I said. "But we may be facing a situation where those words might inspire these guys."

I was right. He went on to read Travis' letter, written when the garrison was besieged by the Mexican army, totally outnumbered, and facing what looked like a hopeless situation. Travis said he would never give up, never surrender, and fight to the end.

Commandancy of the Alamo
Bexar, Feby. 24ᵗʰ, 1836

To the People of Texas and All Americans in the World—
Fellow Citizens and Compatriots
I am besieged with a thousand or more of the Mexicans under Santa Anna. I have sustained a continual Bombardment and cannonade for 24 hours and have not lost a man. The enemy has demanded surrender at discretion otherwise the garrison is to be put to the sword, if the fort is taken. I have answered the demand with a cannon shot, and our flag still waves proudly over the wall. I shall never surrender or retreat. Then, I call on you in the name of Liberty, of patriotism, of everything dear to the American character, to come to our aid with all dispatch. The enemy is receiving reinforcements daily and will no doubt increase to three or four thousand in four or five days. If this call is neglected, I am determined to sustain myself as long as possible and die like a soldier who never forgets what is due his honor and that of his country.

VICTORY OR DEATH.

William Barrett Travis
Lt. Col. Comd't

That hit the players right between the eyes.

Those words—at that juncture—had great meaning to us. Our backs were to the wall. We felt good about what was happening, but we were down four points and two cup matches. We didn't want to lose again.

A few guys reminded us that we had been five points down at Valderrama and almost won. I told them how well they were playing; that they knew the course and all they had to do was play the best they could. They could do it.

Then we went around the room. Everyone who wanted to say something about themselves and the Ryder Cup—wives and girlfriends included—could share something. And everyone did.

"I can't tell you how much it means to be with people who truly care about me," Tiger said. "I go to bed every night with a smile on my face." What an intensely personal, very giving thing to say.

David, too, spoke from the heart. He had made a wonderful speech Wednesday night, and here he was reinforcing his thoughts and feelings again. Only much deeper. He talked about how his point of view toward the Ryder Cup had changed; how he had misspoken about it earlier in the year. The experience of being part of a team now meant so much—it must be similar to having a baby; that you don't know what that's all about until it happens in your life.

Those two gave the team a lot of strength, but so did a lot of others.

Payne said simply, "Don't let them embarrass us again."

And Hal? He stepped up again. He said he was going to forget about mistakes and simply play the kind of golf he believed he was capable of playing. "You know, I've played in the Ryder Cup a few times and I've said it a few times to the press and I am going to say it again to the team: I spent more of my time thinking about not making a mistake. In other words, I have played golf defensively instead of aggressively."

When Hal talks, people listen. It was crunch time and we needed to hear that.

The last person to speak was Robin Love, Davis' wife. She brought up Harvey and what he would have said if he were in the room. "Take dead aim."

The actual words didn't seem nearly as important as the emotions and feelings they were expressing. They had all come from the heart.

Some thought some of my actions that week were over the top, but I wanted to inspire my players to believe in themselves. That was my job. I'm sure Mark James tried to do the same thing for his team in his own way. But whatever he said, there was one thing they didn't know—how emotional we were; how focused this team was.

We were going to have to rewrite history and, as it turned out, Brookline would be there to lend a hand once again. I fell asleep that night thinking about that and what I had said to the press.

I believed in fate.

So did my team.

17.

A MIRACLE

BEST COMEBACKS IN GOLF

Jackie Burke comes from eight back to win 1956 Masters
Arnold Palmer comes from eight back (after two rounds) to win 1960 U.S. Open
Johnny Miller wins 1973 U.S. Open at Oakmont with 63 on Sunday
Nick Faldo defeats Greg Norman to win the 1996 Masters
Billy Casper makes up seven-stroke deficit on Sunday back nine to win
1966 U.S. Open
U.S. Team comes from four points down to win the 1999 Ryder Cup matches

When I walked to the back of the locker room Sunday morning, Tom and Hal were lying there side by side as the trainers stretched them out. It was silent in there—not like most normal mornings in the trailer when everyone is talking about the headlines or the golf course, or telling a joke that won't be repeated once they walk out that door.

I wandered toward them. They would be our first two players off in singles—our two big, steady guns. Tom had drawn Lee Westwood; Hal had Darren Clarke. They would set the tone for us—one that said it was time to rise to the occasion, to come out swinging.

I laid my hand on Tom's chest. "Big boy, we've put you in this position because we believe in you. Go out and do your job."

"I can do it," he said.

Then I turned to Hal. "I can't believe how much you've meant to us this week. You have played incredibly. Keep going."

He gave me one of those closed-mouth smiles of his.

"I'm hurting, I'm really stiff, but I'm going to go out there and do whatever it takes. I'll do it."

I nodded. I couldn't speak. I was too overcome with emotion; so wound up because of what these guys meant to me and what we faced, I simply walked out the door. Then I lost it.

We were emotional from the start—a holdover from Saturday night's talk-around in the team room. We were ready to lay everything we had on the line, ready to redefine the word comeback.

It had been an early night. Everyone was in bed by 11:30, and that next morning Julie went down to the breakfast room to take a quick check of how everyone was feeling. She came in and told me everyone had slept well; they were all positive and ready to go.

Our lineup for the singles was incredible. I mean, it was packed from start to finish, beginning with Tom and Hal and going right down the line—Phil, Davis, Tiger, David, Mark, Steve, Justin, Payne, Jim, and Jeff. It looked even better when we got the draw.

We knew they'd lead off with Clarke and Westwood, but what they did next surprised us. Mark James had kept Jarmo Sandelin, Jean Van de Velde, and Andrew Coltart on the bench the first two days, and we knew from what they were saying they weren't happy about it. Mark said straight out he wanted to win matches and that's why he stuck with his pairings. But when he put Sandelin, Van de Velde, and Coltart off third, fourth, and fifth in singles—matching them against Phil, Davis, and Tiger—we got a twinkle in our eyes.

We thought he would sprinkle them around. But this? To put those three players together that early in the lineup was probably a lot to ask.

All we could think was, "You know what? We can do this."

I'm still mystified as to why Mark did that. Who knows if he made a mistake? He did it the best way he knew. That's about all I can say.

That morning the locker room was quiet and everyone was calm. The players left the locker room with a purpose. And it was never more evident than when we watched Phil. He sat there, deep in his own thoughts, staring into space. Buck asked him what he was doing.

"I'm not going out there," Phil said, "until I'm ready."

No one could ever forget the team shirts we wore that last day. All of our shirts were done by Jeff Rose and it was Julie and I who suggested the design for the final day, a collage of all the team pictures of previous winning American Ryder Cup teams. Reaction was mixed. People either loved them or hated them. Some still refer to them as postcard shirts; others are dying to buy one. And one lucky fan got one—when Tom ripped his off during the celebration and threw it into the crowd.

Julie and I loved them. Here's the thing: they were not meant to be a fashion statement. I had worn a similar shirt on Sunday of the 1995 Masters—the one that had pictures of Bobby Jones on it—and it worked. People loved that shirt and so did I—my heart was in it. We wanted this shirt to mean the same thing to our players—and to remind them whom they were playing for.

It had taken us all of fifteen minutes Saturday night to tentatively settle on our singles lineup. By the time we finished we thought it was perfect. All the players had input, and we strategically put Jim and Payne toward the end where, if we did what we needed to do, that was where it would end.

But back to the beginning. The plan was for Tom to set the tone. What an ideal person to lead off. He was playing well and, when the bar gets raised, Tom focuses even better. Plus, the Ryder Cup means the world to him.

Both he and Hal went out and played like we thought they would. Can you imagine how much confidence that brought to the other players, to watch a guy like Hal, who has been through hell and back, do this thing? We were just lit up with emotion.

Julie and I made it a point to stay with everybody and get them off the first tee. That done, I looked at her and asked, "Who do I go see?"

The board was already bleeding red. We were up in the first six matches—way up. And good things were happening everywhere. I'm listening to Bruce and Bill on the walkie-talkie and Scotty is up in the clubhouse with another one monitoring Sky TV and NBC, keeping us current on the status of the matches, and trying to tell us where we needed to be. We were so wired it was frightening.

I ran out and caught up with Steve, who was playing Jimenez. Their match was close and I told him we were doing great; to keep it up. As always, he made me laugh.

"I'm not hitting the ball that well, but I can out-ugly anybody," he said.

And he did, 2-and-1.

You could see the tension in every player's face. You could see it in their demeanor. The Ryder Cup is no longer a quaint little affair. It's now an event on scale with the Super Bowl—and the momentum was swinging.

Our guys were playing their hearts out. Tom absolutely took over his match against Westwood and was 4-up when he drained an eighteen-foot birdie from the fringe at the thirteenth. He closed out Westwood 3-and-2—for our second point of the day. Davis had already beaten Van de Velde 6-and-5.

We were rewriting history as fast as we could. Hal defeated Clarke, 4-and-2; Phil got Sandelin, 4-and-3; and then Tiger stopped Coltart, 3-and-2.

A 5–0 run? We weren't just feeling, we were believing.

Duval was brilliant, making it 6–0 when he beat Jesper 5-and-4. He was so into the match; I'd never seen him so emotional. He was responding to the crowd's cheers by high-fiving some fans, even signaling for them to yell louder.

The next few matches were all tight—all but Justin's. Furyk was in control of his match. O'Meara's match could go either way. Pate had the lead. Payne was down much of the day, but fought back and squared the match with a twenty-foot putt at fifteen.

Justin had drawn Jose Maria, who is one of the best players under pressure I've ever seen. Then again, so is Justin. Still he was 3-down to Jose Maria through nine holes.

That's when Davis caught up with him and there were tears in his eyes.

"He was not doing good," Davis later said. "I grabbed him by the shoulders and told him it wasn't over. Maybe the people outside the ropes thought this was impossible, but we had faith. We knew he could pull this out."

Davis asked if Justin wanted him to leave, but Justin told him to stay. Of course, Justin lost that hole to go 4-down and joked afterward that he felt like kicking Davis out right then. But they're so close, they're like brothers.

When I heard Davis was there, I got on the walkie-talkie.

"That's perfect. Don't let anyone else go out there. Davis is the only one who can get through to Justin. He's the guy who'll say exactly what he needs to hear. Don't let anyone else go out there. That'll put pressure on him."

Justin couldn't have been in better hands. What Davis said steadied him and raised his composure and his confidence.

Davis knew all Justin had to do was believe. And right then he did. I keep saying golf is unpredictable and this match drove home that point. It changed so suddenly, so dramatically, it was hard to believe.

Jose Maria had been struggling with his driver and it finally cost him; Justin had been struggling with his putter and it came around. The result? Justin won four consecutive holes to square the match— sinking a fifteen-footer at the fourteenth and a thirty-footer at the fifteenth.

I was speechless. This thing was playing out right before our eyes. I was too scared to think. This whole day had unfurled like it had to and my team was playing the most magnificent golf I'd ever seen in my life.

The Europeans didn't win a point until late in the afternoon when Harrington beat Mark 2-and-1. Mark was struggling with his game and battled his heart out, making a great putt at seventeen, but he couldn't hang on and bogeyed the eighteenth.

It was the only time all day we hadn't sustained momentum. And we still led 13–11.

Then in rapid succession, Maggert lost to Lawrie 4-and-3, and Furyk beat Sergio 4-and-3.

I had been with Mark and was scrambling back to seventeen when I heard the roar from fifteen. Furyk had closed out. We had fourteen points.

I got to the back of the seventeenth green and knelt down next to Bruce Edwards and Dave Anderson, the Pulitzer Prize–winning columnist from the *New York Times*. I couldn't speak. I could barely breathe.

My gosh. If Justin can just halve this match, we're going to win the Ryder Cup.

About half of our players and official party were at the green and the other half were at the eighteenth. All we could do was watch.

Justin hit a good second shot and it tried to stay up on the back tier, but there was too much spin on it. It went back down the slope and he had a forty-five-footer. Jose's ball was much closer—twenty-five feet—and his putt was easier.

When he's on, Justin is as good a putter as anyone in golf. He's proven it time after time, especially when he won the 1997 British Open at Royal Troon. His putter had now caught fire on the back nine, allowing him to think he could hole the thirty-five-footer on fifteen which evened the match. Sure, he was putting well, but the putt he now faced was very difficult.

Suddenly my mind started to race. I wondered if someone was watching over us. I mean, here we were on the seventeenth green at The Country Club, the exact place where eighty-six years before, Ouimet had upset Vardon and Ray and put golf on the map in America. The house he grew up in was less than three hundred yards away. It was like a dream.

Fate. It was as though its presence was so heavy, it was dripping from the trees. So much had happened here, and Brookline it seemed took care of its own. It meant so much to history, to Curtis Strange, to me. And now to the Ryder Cup and my team.

I saw Justin lining up his putt and hitting it.

The ball was moving fast. Too fast? It crested the hill, then about eight feet from the hole, I thought it had a chance. The next thing I knew, it just dove right in the hole.

When that putt went in, we erupted. It was the exclamation point to a series of spectacular things that had unfolded all day.

Regardless of what the Europeans thought, the preposterous holing of that putt was the culmination of a day-long chain reaction. Justin threw his arms up. It was pandemonium. A lot of the players and wives and caddies gathered around the green rushed out to celebrate. We were riding a tidal wave that was sweeping across the green.

But it wasn't the end of a dramatic day. It was only the beginning.

18.

VICTORY

MOST SIGNIFICANT RYDER CUP MOMENTS
IN THE LAST TWENTY YEARS

Continental European players added to British Ryder Cup team
Christy O'Connor's 2-iron to final green in 1989 at The Belfry
Lanny Wadkins' wedge to the final green in 1983 at PGA National
Bernard Langer's missed putt on the final green in 1991 at Kiawah Island
Europeans win their first Ryder Cup on U.S. soil in 1987 at Muirfield Village
Davis Love's putt on the final green in 1993 at The Belfry
Justin Leonard's putt on the 17th green in 1999 at The Country Club

We lost it.

Once Justin's ball hit the bottom of the hole, our whole team forgot where we were. Emotions took over and everyone raced toward Justin. Tiger led the charge, leaping so high it was incredible. We were so excited we were out of control.

I was frozen—my mouth wide open. The seventeenth green. Again. To have Justin make *that* putt, I swear, there must have been some predestination. That's why I knew something was going to take care of us—fate.

I don't know how long the celebration lasted, but I remember Justin snapping to and shooing everyone off the green. "Let's get off this green—everybody back."

Jose Maria still had to putt and if he made it, the match would remain all square. He had been waiting the whole time we were celebrating. I'm sure he was upset, wondering when he was going to get his chance. Finally order was restored and he was ready. As he stood over the ball a nearby bus distracted him and he had to back away. Then, incredibly, it happened again.

Jose Maria made a heck of a putt, but he missed . . . so we celebrated again. I walked out to the green, dropped to my knees, and kissed that ground, similar to what Jack did when he kissed Lanny's divot in the 1983 Ryder Cup at Palm Beach Gardens. No one said a thing about Jack. My kiss was another matter all together.

Lanny was standing behind the green as I walked off. He put his arm around my shoulder and shook his head. "You've always had a horseshoe up your ass." We both doubled over.

Jose Maria eventually halved the match with Justin with a brave birdie at the eighteenth, and minutes later, amid the chaos, Payne made the gesture of conceding a putt to Colin on the eighteenth green and lost the final match 1-down.

We rewrote the records, staging the greatest Sunday comeback in Ryder Cup history to win 14½–13½.

We couldn't stop celebrating and neither could the crowd. It was mass confusion. I grabbed my daughter Katherine by the hand and we pushed our way through the crowd to the clubhouse. People were waving huge flags and chanting "U-S-A! U-S-A!" The scene was pure patriotism.

Up at the clubhouse the champagne was flowing. A few players and caddies ran upstairs and climbed onto a small balcony. At one point they wouldn't allow anyone else out there because they had no idea how much weight it would hold. Payne toasted the crowd and the team. Television cameras found Julie and me and Justin. Justin pulled out a cigar—to go with his Diet Coke. The people wouldn't stop cheering. Every player stepped to the edge of the rock wall and the fans went crazy each time. Tom Lehman threw his shirt into the crowd.

Julius Mason of the PGA pulled me aside and said President Clinton was on the phone. I found a quiet spot toward the back of the locker room where I could take the call. The President said he wanted to congratulate the team on a great victory for the United States and that everyone in the White House had watched the telecast and they were going crazy. I really appreciated his call.

The party continued until it was time to get ready for the closing ceremonies. We marched out side by side with the European team, and then Mark and I congratulated each other and all of the players. I was then presented with the Ryder Cup.

Following the ceremony we proceeded to the putting green for the taking of official pictures. As we finished and were about to make our way back to the clubhouse, Bruce Edwards, Linn Strickler, and the rest of the U.S. caddies said they wanted me to follow them for just a moment. About twenty yards away sits a small bronze of Francis Ouimet and his caddie, Eddie Lowery, which means so much to American golf and The Country Club. Bruce looked at me and said, "We want to present you a miniature version of this scene which symbolizes the way we feel about you." I cannot express in words what their gesture meant to me. They were as much a part of this victory as the players.

Meanwhile, Scotty and his wife Julie, and Joe Beck, our friend from Austin, were making their way from the closing ceremonies to the locker room when they were surprised to see Helen Penick and her friend Carol Grigsby. They insisted that Helen and Carol join us for champagne in the team room.

When I saw Helen, I was overwhelmed. I couldn't believe she was there, and somehow it was fitting to have this connection with Harvey at this very moment.

Finally we made our way to the press room and found out the Europeans had made our celebration at the seventeenth green the hot topic. Jose Maria said it was sad to see—such an "ugly picture"—but he didn't make a big deal out of it. He understood the emotions and said we should have exercised better control of them, but made it a point to say that the celebration didn't have anything to do with the outcome.

As Mark James said of us, "They came out screeching. It was quite remarkable."

We made the shots, won the holes, and the crowd got into it. The press came out screeching, too. The first question, from a European journalist, was about our conduct on the seventeenth.

I said we were very sorry and we apologized. We were just so caught up in the moment, there was so much emotion, that it outweighed pragmatism at that point, which is perfectly understandable.

Even Tom Lehman got roasted for being too demonstrative. He spoke for all of us when he said, "What happened on seventeen was unfortunate . . . [but] we all got caught up in the excitement. There was never any ill intent on anybody's part. . . . Obviously, in retrospect, we probably wish we all would have jumped up and down in place instead of running down the side of the green. But I'm not going to apologize for being excited."

I just wish our sincerest apology had been good enough. Some wanted to turn the Ryder Cup into nothing more than an example of a badly timed celebration and overlook everything else. I got more than a few notes demanding that we return the Ryder Cup, and a few more suggesting a lot of not-so-nice things. But I really don't think—as some notes suggested—that we are responsible for the "moral decline" of the matches.

I had to wonder what would have happened if the European team had been in the same situation, on their home soil, trying to make a comeback as we did after losing the two previous Ryder Cup matches. Didn't they ask themselves how emotional they would have been? Put the situation in the same context for them, recreate that scene, and anyone who says the Europeans would not be loud or partisan and supportive are not dealing with reality.

Even those questions couldn't slow us down that night. Back at the hotel it was a nonstop party. We pushed the furniture back to the walls and cut loose. Tequila shots. Beer. Jokes. Cigars. A few tears; a lot of laughs. We had a blast.

Payne was the life of the party, as always. He tossed on a faded melon-colored T-shirt and his favorite loungewear, pants covered with chili peppers, and started dancing on a table. Everyone, it seemed, followed—just not on tables.

Julie and I had a goal that we wanted everyone to have a memorable week, and that certainly was accomplished. We sat there watching their faces and listening to all the stories and it was so satisfying. They were celebrating a miracle—one they had performed as a team.

As I looked around the room, I realized how much everyone meant to me.

Justin. He's got a huge heart and a load of talent. Has anyone ever gone from such despair to such jubilation in the space of six holes? He's fun, he's playful, and he's a kid, but with a killer instinct. And those owl eyes of his . . . well, you saw them in all the pictures. Now Julie calls him "Francis," after Francis Ouimet.

Hal. From the beginning he was the backbone of the team. His actions and deeds and his rock-solid play displayed the conviction of a veteran which we so admired. His time as captain will come soon.

Payne. He was always going to be the most demonstrative. We miss him so much—his leadership, his passion. Payne enjoyed his finest year in 1999 when he won the U.S. Open at Pinehurst and made our team. I'm proud to have had the chance to be his captain.

Jim. I can't say enough about him. He can adapt his game anywhere and he's probably one of the soundest players America has at this point. His contribution got overlooked because he closed out his match just before Justin's putt. It could have been the other way.

Steve. Everybody loved being around him. He's a hell of a player and even though he wasn't playing his very best, he was damned good. And his pairing with Tiger? I just wish we'd tried it sooner. He kept *everybody* loose.

Phil. What a talent. I'll never forget how disconsolate he was over his putting that first day. Then he changed putters and played extremely well after that. He just lacked confidence on the greens. He's such a magnificent player, and I'm really looking forward to the day when he wins his first of many majors.

Tom. I admire him so very much. Certain players simply exude authority and leadership. He had the respect of all of his teammates. We had confidence in his ability to get us off to the start we needed so badly on Sunday. He delivered.

Tiger and David. What more can I say about two of the best players in the world? They played their hearts out, and what they said to the team touched all of us. I know they will play a major role for the U.S. in future Ryder Cup competitions. Certainly playing in his first Ryder Cup gave David a different perspective, and golfers everywhere in this country were inspired by his spirit.

Jeff. No one hits it straighter, and he and Hal made a great team. His game is so dependable it makes him a perfect partner for team competition. He loves playing in the Ryder Cup for his country as much as anyone.

Mark. He had a career year in 1998 and, as I can attest, winning a major, or in his case two, absolutely drains you. He came to the matches struggling with his game, but nearly got the job done against Harrington.

Davis. I've got a great kinship with him, and there's a lot more to it than admiration. He's one of those guys who'll give you everything—just take however many pints of blood you want.

Buck and Leaky. It was comforting to have two of my best friends at my side during this emotional week. I benefited from their experience and wise counsel, and the team loved being with them.

And the wives and girlfriends? I've talked about how hard Julie worked on the preparations. All the girls make great personal sacrifices for their husbands. You can't imagine what a wonderful feeling it is to do so well for your family and your spouse. It's part of an intrinsic value of Ryder Cup week. I don't think anyone understands that—at least anyone from the outside. They're such a huge part of that week and always will be.

When everything calmed down, Hal and Payne talked until the wee hours. Mostly about the Ryder Cup and life. Payne said he wanted Hal to be one of his two assistants when his chance as captain rolled around. Paul Azinger would be the other. That won't happen now, but we saw Payne in his finest hour. I know that when Hal and Paul hopefully take their turns as captain, Payne will be watching.

Julie and I were exhausted. So were a lot of the players. I guess we stayed up well past midnight before turning in.

Everyone fell asleep smiling, still celebrating the miracle that will live forever in our hearts.

19.

ONE APOLOGY IS ENOUGH

TOUGHEST LOSSES

Roberto DeVicenzo 1968 Masters
Jackie Pung signs incorrect scorecard to lose the 1957 Women's U.S. Open
Ben Hogan 1955 U.S. Open at Olympic
Ed Sneed 1979 Masters
Scott Hoch 1989 Masters
Doug Sanders 1970 British Open
Sam Snead 1939 and 1947 U.S. Opens
Ken Venturi 1956 Masters
Arnold Palmer 1966 U.S. Open
Any one of the majors Greg Norman narrowly lost
John Van de Velde, 1999 British Open

About a week after we got home the phone rang. It was Mark James.

He told me how well the U.S. team had played, then got to the real reason for the call. He was about to bring up three issues to the European press and wanted me to know about it.

"I want you to know that this is not about losing," he said. "It is not sour grapes or anything like that."

Mark made three assertions. One was that Payne was seen or overheard giving advice to a player. Another was that when Andrew Coltart lost his tee shot on the ninth hole he was sent off in the wrong direction to look for it, and when the ball was found after the time limit the two marshals there were seen giving each other high fives. The third was that our players had intentionally incited the crowd.

It was not a long-winded conversation. He said what he wanted to say and we didn't converse after that. We exchanged thank you notes as a common courtesy, but no harsh words were in those letters.

But as he talked, my heart sank. I was not expecting anything like this.

We were still trying to recover from the emotions of Sunday. Congratulations were pouring in. I had even taken the replica of the Ryder Cup to my daughter Claire's second-grade show-and-tell at St. Andrews Episcopal School the day I got back. Strange, but four years earlier, I'd walked into my daughter Katherine's second-grade class there with my green jacket from my second Masters.

We took a lot of pictures with the kids, but one thing they wanted to know was "Are you more famous than the President?" Well, no. But it almost felt like it at that point.

The other big question? "Do you know Tiger?" It doesn't matter how old they are, everyone wants to know that.

I was stunned by Mark's call which, in essence, suggested that we had choreographed the last day. As if we could go out to the crowd and say, "This is exactly the way it's going to unfold." We were out there trying not to get beat in our own country. In Boston, no less. His assertions were . . . well, not true. The golf we played energized the crowds, not the other way around.

You're going to accuse Payne Stewart of passing information to a player? That galls me. And assert that two marshals high-fived each other after sending Coltart in the wrong direction? And we incited the cheering?

I had to call Payne, Tom, and Mark. They were playing in the Dunhill Cup the following week and I didn't want them to be surprised by reporters. And I checked out the first two allegations myself.

I found Payne and asked him if he had coached anybody or offered any advice to one of our players. He said it was preposterous; he wouldn't do that.

Then, he said, "Wait a minute, I did say something to Justin one time. I said, 'Get your head out of your ass,' so if that constitutes advice, I guess I'm guilty."

That was my last conversation with Payne and it ended with a big laugh.

The charge against the marshals seemed outrageous, too. I called the official who worked Coltart's match with Tiger, David Price. David is the pro at Bent Tree Country Club, just outside Dallas, and he said that wasn't right. The European fans actually sent the search party in the wrong direction. Plus, there was an official from the Spanish Golf Federation working that match, too, and she didn't raise an objection.

And David went over the time limit for what should have been a five-minute search. "I tried to give it some leeway. We didn't need any incidents over that."

Also, because so much was being written about Jose Maria's line being "trampled" on seventeen, I wanted to investigate that situation as well. I called Jim Deaton, the pro at Bay Hill, who was the official with Justin and Jose Maria. He stated emphatically that no one crossed into Jose Maria's line. He was responsible for making certain of that, and it was a hard job with that mass confusion.

Maybe the most troubling of Mark's accusations was the idea that our players were inciting the crowd. Mark described it with a soccer analogy, saying that if a player on your side incites the crowd, then your team receives a penalty. He said a number of our players were guilty of whipping up the crowd.

What I saw was a team getting excited about the way it was playing, and the fans reacting. It wasn't personal. We were playing extremely well and the crowd was responding to it with their cheers and support.

We just played unbelievably that day. The superior quality of our golf was simply amazing.

People need to understand that there was nothing personal meant toward the European players. We all have a deep respect for them—and their talent. We had to play like hell just to get back into the matches.

Not enough was written about the great golf we played that day. Too many reporters and columnists chose to concentrate on the emotions and the controversy.

They're the ones asking if the Ryder Cup is too intense, too over the top. I think the media as a whole has to shoulder some of the responsibility for the mindset. Players from both teams are chastised personally and mercilessly in the media when they fail. We played near-flawless golf that final day, yet it wasn't the focus of most of the stories I read.

Then Mark called.

The conversation stung, but after I talked with my players I didn't think much more about it until Mark's book—*Into the Bear Pit*—came out. The accusations were all there. The celebration. Payne. The marshals. The theory that we incited the fans. For the sake of peace, let's just say, I disagree with a lot of his book. It's so disappointing, and it does hurt like the devil when things like that are written about the team.

Many factors affected our performance on Sunday. I'll take a small measure—a very small measure—of credit. But these guys played inspired golf. And a captain can only inspire them so much. These guys did it for themselves. They did it for each other.

Losing twice in a row had everything to do with it, too. It had everything to do with their effort, their belief, their drive, their search within themselves, the fact they almost did it at Valderrama. It exploded out of them.

In more than a few instances fans were guilty of improper behavior—especially some of the things that were said to Colin. We've apologized for two things—the actions by a few unruly fans and the celebration at seventeen. It seems as though we will continue to be asked to apologize for seventeen for a long time. But other than that it was one team outplaying the other. That's what it boiled down to.

Nobody will ever be able to take away the golf that we played. And as Hal and Tom and a few others have said, nobody will ever be able to remove the joy we felt from that victory. We did what we had to do. Our team played brilliantly. But to say the game is in danger because of our actions is absurd.

I don't mean to sound as though I'm trying to get the last word, but a few things rankled me about the Ryder Cup that I'm going to get off my chest. Then I'm going to let go and forget about them.

I have to say, unequivocally, the European team used the tactic of slow play to the fullest extent. The pace was excruciatingly slow, to the point that we nearly didn't get finished the first night. Ask Davis, ask Tom. Many times the Europeans were the last ones to get to the next tee and they seemed to deliberate more than usual.

Saturday afternoon Phil was so frustrated at the eleventh tee that he hit his drive before the Europeans arrived. Davis and Justin were equally upset Friday when Davis told Colin and Lawrie, "Look, we have to get on with these matches. You can't slow play us forever."

Usually you have forty-five seconds to hit your shot once you get to the ball. This is the rule on the PGA Tour, but it all goes out the window in the Ryder Cup. It is understood by both sides that they will monitor the situation as best they can, but no one wants to start an international incident, so slow play often occurs.

If they're looking for ways to make the matches better, then speeding up the pace of play is my number one suggestion. Somebody has got to do something about it. There were only four matches going on at a time and we still almost didn't finish one night because of the pace of play.

I have a feeling the slow play was designed to throw us off our pace. Maybe they tried to be the last ones off the greens to counteract any crowd noise, but whatever the reason, it's safe to say that there was a concerted effort to slow things down. I find it interesting that Mark James addressed the issue in his book, but accused *our* team of slow play. It seemed to us that just the opposite was true.

Mark took several individual American players to task in his book, and I especially have a problem with his questioning Tom Lehman's moral character. Tom is one of the most solid people we have in this game and clearly doesn't deserve being dragged through the mud. Personal attacks have no place in golf.

I suppose some people think this Ryder Cup was played to fit some personal agenda on our part, but there was nothing personal about it. We wanted our team to win, period. The Ryder Cup is three days. It's totally unpredictable, as we are reminded every time we play. We got the best of them this time, but if we held the matches again in another week, they might get the best of us.

We played better than they did on the last day and we deserved to win. They need to move on just like we did in 1995 and 1997 when we lost. You congratulate the other team and you move on. To say that the Americans have tarnished the game and endangered the future of golf is a bitter statement.

We need to rise above this whole thing. Mark had his observations; we saw things much differently. Let's leave it at that.

I certainly know what to expect at the next Ryder Cup: loud, partisan crowds, lots of emotion, and spirited play. Curtis knows that and he'll be prepared. So will his team. Curtis is the best man we can have in that situation.

When Mark brought all of this up, I sought out the esteemed writer Herbert Warren Wind. We've been friends a long time and I wanted to know how our Sunday at The Country Club might have compared to the day Ouimet won there in 1913.

"Do you think the crowd got as boisterous?" I said, hoping for a clear-cut answer.

"Comparatively so," he said.

On that day, fans sensed something completely different happening at the staid old country club. It was a feeling of excitement they'd never before felt in American golf—an innocence that carried "the kid across the street" to the U.S. Open title and popularized golf in the States. People were stepping on each other to get near Ouimet amid a chorus of cheers and yells.

Not long ago I was flipping through an advance copy of a book to be published which contained the *New York Times* story written about that eventful day. I have read accounts from several authors about what happened, but this one was different. I got chills and the hairs on the back of my neck stood up.

The similarities between what transpired on that rainy afternoon and on our Sunday were incredible. I couldn't believe it. I cannot do it justice by trying to explain it, so I'll let you judge for yourself:

> *The scenes of jubilation on the home green after the match had been won were, therefore, but natural expressions of pride and pleasure at Ouimet's success in retaining a championship for America which was considered earlier in the week destined to cross the Atlantic.*
>
> *Thousands of dripping, rubber-coated spectators massed about Ouimet, who was hoisted to the shoulders of those nearest him, while cheer after cheer rang out in his honor. Excited women tore bunches of flowers from their bodies and hurled them at the youthful winner; hundreds of men strove to reach out and shake his hand.*
>
> *Ray and Vardon, whose fight for the open championship brought out the possibilities of Ouimet as a golfer, were not forgotten in the celebration of the victory. Each Englishman got a three times three* (hip-hip-hooray) *before the parade started for the dressing quarters, where the recent competitors changed to dry clothing for the presentation of the medals and other prizes.*
>
> *During the ceremony, in which Secretary John Reid, Jr., acted as master of ceremonies, both Ray and Vardon took the opportunity to praise Ouimet as a sportsman and golfer. Ray said*

*that Ouimet had played the best golf during the four-day strug-
gle that he had ever seen in America and that it had been an
honor to play with him and no dishonor to lose to him. Vardon
brought cheers from the gallery when he frankly stated that they
had never had a chance to win with Ouimet, during the playoff, because he'd played better golf and never gave them an opening at one of the eighteen holes. He congratulated Ouimet and
America on the victory and proved a popular speechmaker as
well as golfer. Secretary Reid, in awarding the championship
medal to Ouimet, the trophy to the Woodland Club of Auburn-
dale, Mass., which he represented, and cash prizes to Vardon
and Ray, took occasion to apologize "in a slight way" as he put
it, for the outbursts of cheering at inopportune times.*

*This was a delicate reference to a feature of today's play
which is quite likely to be a subject of international comment by
the golfing contingents of England and the United States. The
management of the tournament has been the subject of much
praise, but today the gallery several times violated the keen ethics
of the sports, by cheering wildly whenever Ouimet gained a
point. The same outbursts occurred yesterday, but Ouimet was
then playing with George Sargent, who had no chance for first
place in the final half of his round.*

*Today was different, for both Ray and Vardon were playing
shots either just before or after Ouimet and it was plainly evident that these outbreaks annoyed them. Approaching the seventeenth hole, Ray deliberately stopped in the midst of a swing and
refused to play until the cheering ceased. This action of the
gallery had little or no effect on the results of the match, but a
number of golfers publicly voiced regret that cheering like that at
boat races or football games should have occurred, although they
realized and stated that it was impossible to check these national
outbursts of enthusiasm when Ouimet made particularly good
plays.*

Strange, isn't it? A bit eerie, perhaps. Two spectacular American golf moments at the same spot—separated by eighty-six years. Two improbable events celebrated with unbelievable passion and emotion.

Ouimet didn't need to spend the rest of his life apologizing.

Neither should I.

Neither should my team.

20.

A HOLE IN THE HEART

MOST COLORFUL PLAYERS

Max Faulkner
Walter Hagen
Jimmy Demaret
Lee Trevino
Peter Jacobsen
Tommy Bolt
Doug Sanders
Payne Stewart

Tears were falling down Tom Lehman's cheeks as he stepped to the microphone. His lips were quivering. He paused to gather his thoughts and heaved a deep sigh.

Then, he spoke from his heart.

"He was a very emotional guy," Lehman said. "He loved to laugh and he was not ashamed to cry. I'm not going to be ashamed of my tears this morning, and neither should you."

We weren't. About fifty players and a thousand others had gathered at the first tee at Champions Golf Club that morning to say goodbye. Feelings of loss, of grief, of shock were washing over us as we sat in folding chairs on the tee box and waited for the lone bagpiper to make his way down the fairway. A fog had settled in over that tiny part of Houston that morning, adding to the numbness everyone felt and the emptiness no words could explain.

I, like everyone there, had loved Payne Stewart like a brother. Our grief was deeper than anyone could imagine. It was like someone had torn a hole in our hearts.

He had just come through such a fabulous year. He'd won his second U.S. Open. We'd won the Ryder Cup and shared so much—so many intimate moments with the team and our wives.

Now this.

Our world was shattered.

I was on my way to the Austin Golf Club when my phone rang on October 25, 1999. It was Julie.

"Honey, you have to come home," she said. "There's news breaking on CNN. There's an airplane that's in trouble coming out of Orlando and I have a terrible feeling we know someone on the plane."

I turned the car around and drove home. When I walked in the door Julie had just gotten off the phone with Amy and Phil Mickelson, who had told her Payne was on the plane.

It was chilling watching that plane drift across the sky. When official confirmation came in we were stunned beyond belief. Because we were getting so many calls from reporters, Tom Kite, Scotty, and I decided the best thing would be to hold an impromptu news conference to express our grief and field questions. That was one of the hardest press conferences I've ever been through.

We spoke of our affection for Payne, and about how the players on the PGA Tour are really like a big family. We live together week in and week out and have strong feelings for one another. We all suffered with Stuart Appleby when his wife, Renay, was tragically killed in an auto-pedestrian accident. With so many players flying in private jets, this could have happened to any of us.

The accident happened the Monday of Tour Championship week, just as the top thirty players were traveling to Houston. Most of the Ryder Cup team was playing there and I was planning to go down and visit the players and Jackie Burke. Suddenly I felt an urgency. I wanted to be with my players.

I was trembling the whole time. When I got there I saw the saddest, most bewildered bunch of guys I'd ever seen. They were so lost. It was just so damn sad. Every time we saw a picture of Payne on the news, it hurt more.

Everyone was in shock and disbelief. They didn't know what to do. Their minds were elsewhere, but they had a tournament to play.

The service on the first tee Thursday morning helped. Until then we'd spoken to each other individually. Here, on the morning play would begin, we gathered for the first time as a group to share our grief.

Tom Lehman's tribute was one of the most moving that I've ever witnessed. Tom is possessed of a rock-solid belief in our Lord. He said some things that a lot of us were incapable of saying; he showed great strength and character, and gave us comfort.

Play was postponed on Friday and almost everyone flew to Orlando for services at Payne's church. Tracey showed incredible strength, speaking at her own husband's funeral. We felt so bad for her and their children, Aaron and Chelsea.

When Julie and I saw Tracey, the first thing she said was, "I'm so thankful for that week we spent together" (at the Ryder Cup).

Once again it seemed that we were incapable of saying all we wanted, but everyone was able to express their sorrow.

He touched us in so many ways, we'll never be the same.

21.

GOLF IN THE NEW MILLENNIUM

THINGS I WISHED I'D DONE IN GOLF

Won a British Open
Met Bobby Jones
Hit a better 2-iron on the 71st hole at the 1975 U.S. Open
Had a dry grip on my shot to the 72nd hole in the 1989 Masters
Taken better care of "Little Ben"
Visited more golf courses during my travels
Found a designated driver!

Do you ever wonder where golf is headed? I do.

The game is exploding. It's been on the rise for a long while, but suddenly it has taken off like one of those hypersonic planes they say will one day vault us from Sydney to London in thirty minutes.

Could we really see a 9,000-yard course or the day when 400-yard drives are routine? Don't laugh. It may not be that improbable.

Just look at technology. We used to play with forged irons, steel shafts, and wound balls. Now look at our options. Manufacturers and designers are pushing all limits—testing the rules of the game, the playability of courses, the sensibilities of golfers everywhere. Steel or graphite? Metal or antiquated persimmon? Long putter? Perimeter weighted cavity-back clubs? A new—but illegal—Callaway ERC II driver?

What's happening here?

The golf ball? Everyone's looking for an edge. Spin. Distance. Maneuverability.

Jackie Burke laughs about the commercials and infomercials on The Golf Channel.

"You're watching it and here comes this great ball, then a great club," he says. "The ball is going to give you twenty more yards. Then this club claims it's going to give you twenty more yards.

"Hey, I've picked up forty yards and I haven't left my living room chair!"

I don't think that you can *buy* a game. There are no quick fixes in golf. But there are rules. And it seems to me that technology is forcing the issue.

The late Karsten Solheim went to court in the mid-1980s over the square grooves controversy. The USGA had banned clubs in the past because they did not conform to specifications, but this was the first substantial, legal challenge to their authority.

In 1999, Callaway announced it would sell a new driver—the ERC II. Although the driver is approved by the R&A, the USGA does not deem it legal. The club wasn't submitted to the USGA for testing, but that didn't matter because it wouldn't have passed the conforming tests. The company knew it and said they would sell it anyway.

And Arnold Palmer, who had just signed with Callaway, supported the company's decision. This was a shocking turn of events.

Over the years there have been disagreements. There was the 1921 British Open at St. Andrews. Jock Hutchison won in a playoff and his clubs were scrutinized by the R&A because officials thought the markings on his irons were too deep. They claimed his clubs produced excessive backspin and the topic produced lively discussions.

But this action by Callaway was something different. A lot of people saw this as a train wreck that had been coming for a long time.

It raises the question of who sets the rules? Who sets the policy? The USGA? The R&A? Manufacturers? I believe the R&A and USGA should work together. They have had certain differences, but they've always worked them out.

This one created a fissure. One manufacturer thumbed its nose at the rules. Arnold sided with them.

What's next? I'm just very disappointed. Golf has survived too long playing under an accepted set of rules.

I will say that I think the rules have become too complex. I wish there were some way to make them easier for people to understand. What it all boils down to is: Play the ball as it lies, hit it in the hole, add it up. And do it with equipment that is legal.

Three ingredients that have always made golf so fascinating are the players, the manufacturers, and the ruling authorities. Basically golf is a traditional game and people pretty well understand that you play by the rules and play by the honor you can summon within you. If you knowingly break the rules there's swift and severe punishment, and it's been that way throughout the history of the game. Conscience plays a big role in golf. If someone sees you cheat, that's the worst consequence that can fall upon a golfer. Immediately you're an outcast and there are no good graces by which you can return. That's a heavy price to pay.

People have played by the rules for more than 250 years. It's a game that, hopefully, players honor with a code of ethics. Now there's a serious threat to the rules and the stability they've provided since the Honorable Company of Edinburgh Golfers adopted them in 1744. Ten years after they were drafted, St. Andrews and the R&A became the seat of the ruling authority of the game. The USGA was formed in 1894 and started on shaky ground. It took them a while to rule in concert with the R&A, but overall they've done a spectacular job of protecting the integrity of the game and making their rulings for all golfers.

I know the argument is going to be made that this new driver is for average golfers—not professionals—but that doesn't matter. It's something that's going to tear the game apart. The question to me is, Are you going to abide by an accepted set of rules, or do you think that matters at all?

No matter what happens, golf courses are at risk. Architects have struggled for years over the question of, How do we create a fair test for everyone given this technology?

On one end of the spectrum is Tiger. He's the prototype of every golfer's imagination. Fifteen or twenty years ago they said this person would come along. They just didn't know how well he would putt and chip. But it's not just Tiger. It's a whole host of talented, serious young athletes who have benefited from better teaching at a younger age. They're more prepared and their bodies are stronger. The myth of avoiding weightlifting has been thrown out the window; people used to believe it wasn't beneficial for golfers.

And just look at all the things young golfers have at their disposal today. They have the best golf clubs ever made. They're more consistent, the components in the head design are more forgiving, and the metals are better. Shafts are now produced in a variety of materials and it seems that a new one hits the market every week.

The length of the club is a huge part of the emphasis on power. Not long ago, forty-three inches was the accepted standard for a driver. Now it's forty-five inches and longer.

Advances in agronomy are also changing the game. New grasses are being developed that are more consistent, making greens putt truer than ever. It all results in lower scores.

Even with all this technology, most top golfers in the world still play forged blades. They feel they have more control and can move the ball around and at different heights. But for the average or higher handicap golfer, game-improvement technology has vastly increased the margin for error and made the game more appealing, more fun.

But if you put all of these things in a hat, shake the ingredients up, and throw them out on the table, something's got to give. A golfer these days has been afforded every possible way to improve—but that doesn't include reshaping or ignoring the rules.

The ruling bodies aren't the only ones facing tough questions, though. Players are, too.

When I joined the PGA Tour we had no more than thirty-two tournaments. We started in January, but when October rolled around that was it. No more tournaments. You basically had two and a half months off, or you could play one or two overseas events. Early in my career I did go to Japan, Australia, and England, but even then I still had two months off.

Now a top player's schedule has to be segmented. He has to play in clusters. There's a tournament every week on almost every continent and players have to decide what's going to be best for their game; how they can maximize their potential; where to put their best efforts. It's a lot more complex than it used to be.

With the majors and the World Golf Championships and the Ryder Cup and President's Cup, the top players in the game are already committed to more than a dozen events before the year starts. Jack Nicklaus, Tom Watson, and Lee Trevino always built their schedules around the majors and most players still do. The system is stressed with all of these extra events and global travel, however.

I don't care if you're flying on a private jet, you're body is still taxed. It takes a lot out of you. I think there are just too many tournaments on all the tour schedules. The PGA Tour has what—forty-five? That's just seven weeks off. I think the struggle for quality fields is going to get tougher.

Nearly all tournaments are lucrative, so much so that money has become secondary in a player's decision to play an event. And although the PGA Tour has no appearance fees, the best players can go anywhere in the world for huge sums.

Before 1980, I don't think I ever got more than $40,000 to play overseas, but I do remember the 1976 Irish Open. I got a $25,000 appearance fee to play and, even though I won, I felt like I had extra pressure on me to perform well. The numbers today are mind-boggling. Tiger is being lured to tournaments around the world with seven-figure offers, but given what he has accomplished and his impact on the game, he's probably worth whatever he's paid.

Golf is truly a global game now and the best players will have to balance their schedules to protect against wearing themselves out. To compete against the best in the world you must be sharp both mentally and physically.

The face of golf is changing. It's reaching new people and different parts of the world. And people worldwide are seeing how wonderful it is; how it can occupy their attention, their focus, their minds for a lifetime. Young or old, you never stop learning about it.

Gary Player was the first golfer to bring the game to a global audience, then Greg Norman and Nick Price picked up the mantle. Now it's getting more attention around the world because of the success of wonderful players like Vijay Singh from Fiji, Native American Notah Begay III, and Paraguay's Carlos Franco.

At the same time, something very important is disappearing—the caddie.

Caddies used to be a vital part of the game, and many players like Nelson and Hogan grew up caddying. Now with the proliferation and financial boon of carts, a lot of people have never played using a caddie. And if you haven't, you should.

When you have a caddie you really feel the game. Caddies know golf through and through and they know how to read people. They usually tell you the truth whether you like it or not and they love the game. Plus, I do believe God has given them a special sense of humor. They are so funny. Some have an impish humor, while the Scots are extremely dry.

If you let them, they can teach you much about the game. My good friend Bobbie Millen, who caddies for me in Great Britain, Scotland, and Ireland, is a fine player himself and he encouraged my interest in the history of the game. He knew I loved it and was always helping me deepen my knowledge.

And, they have hunches. Where would I have been without Carl in 1995? He knew what was wrong with my swing and fixed it. We're like a team, as are so many players and caddies. Look at what Tiger has done with Steve Williams on his bag. There's a chemistry there.

Caddies are integral on the Tour, but club caddies are important, too. It's hard to see so many clubs going away from them. I think back to how much all those Augusta caddies—men like Carl—have meant to every golfer who's played there. Not just those playing in the Masters.

My first caddie there was a man named Luke and he was quite an experience. Talk about telling it like it is. During one of my first practice rounds I had about 180 yards to the green at number five. I looked over and Luke had his hand on the 5-iron.

"Luke, I'm not sure if I can quite get there," I said.

He didn't blink. "Well, hit the 4-iron then!"

The best ones have such great instincts. And if I had gone with Carl's instinct, I might have won another Masters.

In 1987, I hit it down the right side at seventeen on the final day. Carl wanted me to go with a pitching wedge for my second shot. The pin was back right and I studied it a little, but decided to hit a light 9-iron. I pulled it three to four feet off my line, and it went a little too far and I had a tough pitch. It took me three to get down and I bogeyed. If I'd hit the wedge I could have hit anywhere short of the hole, and the worst I would have made was a par four.

Looking back, he was right. I finished one shot out of the playoff between Larry Mize and Norman.

And Bobbie? If I'd listened to him, I might have carried off a Claret Jug. He was always saying, "We've got plenty of holes to play. Dig in. Everybody's going to have trouble today." That was his way of trying to calm me down. I don't know if I ever really did.

If we lose caddies in this game, we're going to lose a vestige of the game that will never be able to be appreciated again.

And if we lose this battle with technology? I worry about the great courses that would no longer hold majors. They're all at risk.

My mind always drifts to Merion. The course is marvelous and you play it with your instincts. There are absolutely no yardages on sprinklers, no 150-yard bushes, and the wicker baskets on the flagpoles make it difficult to gauge any breeze that may be blowing.

It's real golf there—golf like Hogan loved to play.

One time someone asked him if he believed in yardages.

"No," Hogan said. "It would deprive me of the pleasure of a well executed shot."

In a way, technology may eventually deprive us of a few more wonderful things in the game, too.

If Dr. MacKenzie or Donald Ross or any of the other great architects came back now, I wonder what would they think of carts, equipment, and what they've done to their courses. I never knew them, but I've studied their lives, their courses, and their thoughts on the game. I think they'd take a dim view of it. For centuries golf has had a strong enough backbone to hold onto its beliefs. I hope it continues.

EPILOGUE

Know what I can see from my front porch? The end of my driveway.

That's a pretty relaxing view at this stage of my life.

The kids' toys are where they left them the night before—or maybe the night before that. The cicadas are buzzing in the sprawling old oak trees. Our house has a constant stream of visitors and a warm, welcoming feel.

We live just a few blocks from my childhood home on Bridle Path and every so often I drive by to see if I can see any bald spots on the lawn—a sure sign of a new generation of Little Leaguers in the house. I think back to those baseball games, the catcher's mitt, and the windows we broke chipping golf balls. I remember how Charlie and I would sneak into Bonnie's room and rearrange all the things we weren't supposed to touch. I think about Mom cooking supper and Dad walking in with clients in tow.

I wonder if kids with purple hands are sitting in that old mulberry tree, stuffing their faces.

I laugh every time I think about how much trouble Charlie and I got into.

When we celebrated his fiftieth birthday, I knew mine wasn't far away. Funny how, as you approach that milestone, which for me was January 11, 2002, you reflect so much more and truly begin to realize what life is all about.

As I look at everything and everyone around me, I realize I owe myself a little bit of a break from the grind as my life kind of takes off in another direction. And Brookline was the turning point.

Nobody has been luckier in life than me. The two Masters. Harvey. Julie and the girls. My family. The Ryder Cup. For me to be captain anywhere would be incredible, but to be captain at Brookline, it meant the world to me. The Ryder Cup is tailored for my heart and my emotions. It was such an incredible week, the whole thing is surreal, even now.

I suspect that that week—the whole captaincy—has affected my play as much as getting older has. I haven't really put a lot of time into my game in the past few years because I put so much of myself into that job for two years. It's not that I had to, it's that I wanted to. It still amazes me how Tom was able to play so well during his captaincy. I'm just not made that way.

Julie and I spent so much time working on details, trying to make certain everything would be perfect for the players, there just wasn't time for my game. Or a lot of other things.

Ever since we got home from Boston, I've immersed myself in my family and our architecture business. I've played very little and even skipped the British Open qualifying this year—and it was at St. Andrews.

Home is where my heart is right now—with all four of my girls who bring me such joy.

Where would I be without Julie? We've shared so many moments, been through so many things, it's hard to describe.

And the kids? Katherine, our oldest at fourteen, is so smart, so sweet. She was with us at the Ryder Cup and got to experience the whole thing—she's seen the Backstreet Boys three times now in concert. She's a good little artist and a good athlete. Right now she plays softball and volleyball, but I suppose one of these days I'd like her to hit a golf ball or two. Claire, our middle daughter who is almost ten, is so much fun. She's like a jumping bean, very athletic, and has a heck of a little spirit. She's a fighter. And both of them dote on little Anna Riley, who just turned four and has a sweet disposition.

Each summer we head to our beach house in California near where Julie's parents live. I'm lucky to be so close to my in-laws Sue and Warren Forrest and Julie's sister and brother and their five children—all daughters. We all spend a lot of time together and, as you can imagine, the beach is quite a scene with all eight girls bouncing around.

I know, everyone's children are special, but I think it's magnified when you're a late father like I am. I traveled the Tour for many years in sort of a one-dimensional way—single or married without children. Now, my life is the kids.

Once you have children you really do see things differently. You realize how short a time you have with them, so you want to spend all the time you can with them. You want to love and nurture them. You want to be the best parents you can be—and believe me, I had great role models in Mom and Dad.

As far as business goes, getting the new Austin Golf Club up and running has consumed a lot of my time and energy. I go out there and visit that landscape and just let my mind go. It's so beautiful, so rewarding.

During the 2000 presidential campaign, I lent a hand to my candidate and friend—George W. Bush. I campaigned a bit with my golf clubs and was supposed to be with him when he was nominated, but the weather got me. I watched him accept the nomination in Philadelphia on television in Pittsburgh, where my plane was grounded, but Julie and I were both able to be with him on December 13, 2000, when he made his official acceptance speech in Austin. And we attended the Inauguration. Since then, Julie and I have been able to visit the White House several times and I was invited to stay there during the 2001 Kemper Open.

You add it all up and my golf game is taking a back seat now. That's fine. I no longer have the desire to go out there and just play, week after week, which is what it takes these days.

I'm playing the Senior PGA Tour now and I'm still tinkering with Little Ben in hopes that I'll find the perfect shaft and regain that old feel. The Senior Tour is a different tour, a different lifestyle, and I'm spending the first year adjusting to new cities, new courses, new restaurants, and two days of pro-ams for first-year players. But it's great to be out here playing against all my old friends and contemporaries like Tom Kite, Lanny and Bobby Wadkins, Tom Watson, Larry Nelson, Hale Irwin, and even Leaky, who won the third senior event he played in after turning fifty last year. Bobby Wadkins won the first one he entered. I'm having fun testing my game again and seeing who has the best stories after all these years.

The nicest thing about our game is all the people you meet, all the places you get to go, and the life you live while you're doing it. The game is a common language to me. It doesn't matter where you play, each golfer meets people in their life who make the difference, whether it's their parents or teachers or a Harvey. Whoever they are, those people put golf in your soul.

And as you go through life I think it gets simpler. When you get down to it, you have your family and your friends and a chance to work at something you love. I've had golf in my life, but I've been truly blessed beyond that with my wonderful family and outstanding friends, who provide counsel and guidance and are there no matter what.

As Bobby Jones said, a life in friendship is full indeed. And if friendships are man's life treasures, I've had them in abundance. I've talked at length about Scotty, but I've also relied on friends like Brent Buckman, Bobby Kay, Pat Oles, Bill Coore, and Alec Beck. We've shared life, business, and the three main food groups in Texas— chicken fried steak, barbecue, and Mexican food. We've laughed. We've cried. We've grown up together—and now we're watching our children begin their journeys.

Life and golf are intertwined. Where would I be without the game? How would I have met so many wonderful people? And how else could I explain it after the Ryder Cup?

Being there at Brookline with my dad when I was sixteen. Winning the Masters for Harvey. Serving as captain of the Ryder Cup team at the very same course where Francis Ouimet made history.

I keep going back to this, but it's the only explanation. Things happen for a reason. I do believe in fate. That Saturday night in the press room at Brookline, I honestly knew that people were going to read my "good feeling" prediction in the newspaper the next day and think I was crazy.

But I had this feeling.

My whole life has been guided by feelings. They're nothing I can put my finger on. I just know—like I did at Brookline and twice at Augusta. Maybe I learned that from my mother. She was always saying, "Everything is going to be all right, Bennie." She was so upbeat, so encouraging. I always knew everything was going to be all right—I just had to trust.

It's the same way with this book. As you read my thoughts and feelings, I hope you can understand what golf has meant to me. I count my blessings every single day that golf is a part of me because it's been responsible for some of the nicest things that have happened to me—

better things than I could ever have imagined. Two major championships at my favorite course. A total of twenty-two victories worldwide. The opportunity to play on four Ryder Cup teams. The chance of a lifetime to captain a winning one.

After the 1995 Masters, I thought about retiring. I told myself I couldn't do anything that would have any deeper meaning or elicit stronger emotions. It seemed foolish to do anything else after that. And when I asked myself where I was going from there, I didn't know the answer. It was so fulfilling for me, emotionally and professionally. I did it with Julie, my friends, my family. I felt I could never feel that way about anything again.

But in my heart, I realized that I still enjoyed playing. And while I haven't played with the same intensity since, I did captain that Ryder Cup team with it.

I believe golf is timeless and, if you're lucky, you have it with you all your life. It evolves and connects and moves from one time to another, from history to new history, from person to person. From course to course—and back again.

For me, Brookline is as much a part of the fabric of my career as Augusta or Harvey. To captain a Ryder Cup there? It's hard to put that into words.

Brookline meant so much to me personally and I didn't want anyone to know that. Not even my team. I knew if I put those personal feelings on them, they might not have understood. I didn't want them to feel extra pressure, but for me it completed a circle.

My journey as a golfer had begun there with my father. We lost him about a year before the matches, but he and I had talked a lot about it and it made him so very happy that I was going to be captain there.

All those things that make me what I am—an appreciation for history, a passion for architecture and golf—it all started that week in 1968. A sixteen-year-old kid learning about the game and taking the first steps in a long career; a proud father walking the fairways, nurturing his son and that dream.

As that final press conference was coming to a close at Brookline that Sunday, a reporter asked what I would have asked Dad, if he could have been there. That got me.

I broke down, burying my face in my hands. Someone tried to move to the next question, but I was adamant. I wanted to answer the question—and I did as tears rolled down my cheeks.

A beautiful harness racing track used to run along the right side of the first fairway and crossed the eighteenth. When we were there in '68, Dad would walk along that track, agonizing over every shot I hit.

I blinked away the tears and let my mind wander.

I could still see Dad walking across that track.

He was there that afternoon just as sure as Harvey was. Both of them guiding me, watching over me, helping me live out my dream—still nurturing that passion they gave me for the game.

MORE OF BEN'S LISTS

PIONEER TWENTIETH-CENTURY GOLF TEACHERS

Harvey Penick

Stewart Maiden

Seymour Dunn

Bob Toski

Jack Burke

Claude Harmon

Eddie Merrins

Tommy Armour

John Redman

FAVORITE SCOTTISH GOLF COURSES

St. Andrews
Muirfield
Gleneagles King
North Berwick
Turnberry

FAVORITE AUSTRALIAN GOLF COURSES

Royal Melbourne
Kingston-Heath
Commonwealth
Metropolitan
Barwon Heads

FAVORITE GREENS AT AUGUSTA

#5
#14
#10
#7
#9
#17
#1

FAVORITE MASTERS

1995
1984
1972 (my first)
1986
1975

BEST AUSTIN TEX-MEX

Cisco's
El Patio
Maudies
El Rancho
Nuevo Leon
El Arroyo

BEST PLAYERS IN GOLF HISTORY

Jack Nicklaus
Tiger Woods
Bobby Jones
Ben Hogan
Byron Nelson
Sam Snead

TOUGHEST RECORDS IN GOLF

Jones Grand Slam
Nicklaus' twenty major championships
Hogan's 1953; Masters, U.S. Open, British Open
Byron Nelson's eleven straight Tour wins
Sam Snead's eighty-one Tour wins
Kathy Whitworth's eighty-eight Tour wins
Tiger Woods' 2000 season

TOUGHEST SHOTS IN GOLF

Driving into a left to right breeze
Long bunker shot
Long shot to the green with trouble across the approach

Long iron from a downhill lie
The next *shot!*

BEST BUNKER PLAYERS

Gary Player
Chi Chi Rodriguez
David Graham
Seve Ballesteros
Tom Watson

BEST DRIVERS

Greg Norman
Nick Price
Hale Irwin
Hal Sutton
Lee Trevino

BEST CLUTCH PLAYERS

Jack Nicklaus
Tom Watson
Tiger Woods
Arnold Palmer
Ben Hogan
Lee Trevino
Bobby Jones

1973 San Antonio Texas Open

1976 Bing Crosby National Pro-Am

1976 Hawaiian Open

1976 Ohio Kings Island Open

1977 Colonial National Invitational

1979 Phoenix Open

1979 Walt Disney World Team Championship (with George Burns)

1980 Anheuser-Busch Classic

1983 Byron Nelson Classic

1984 The Masters

1986 Buick Open

1986 Vantage Tour Championship

1987 USF&G Classic

1988 Doral Ryder Open

1990 Southwestern Bell Colonial

1992 Centel Western Open

1993 Nestle Bay Hill Invitational

1994 Freeport McMoRan Classic

1995 The Masters

BEN CRENSHAW INTERNATIONAL
TOURNAMENT WINS

1976 Irish Open

1981 Mexican Open

1988 World Cup; Individual Champion

1967 & 1969 Texas State Junior Amateur Champion

1968 National Jaycee Junior Champion

1971 & 1972 Eastern Amateur Champion

1971 & 1973 Southern Amateur Champion

1971, 1972,* 1973 NCAA Individual Champion
   (*co-champion w/Tom Kite)

1971, 1972 Member NCAA Championship Team (University of Texas)

1972 Trans-Mississippi Amateur Champion

1972 Porter Cup Amateur Champion

1972 Eisenhower World Cup Amateur Team

1972 Texas State Amateur Champion

1973 Northeast Amateur Champion

1973 Sunnehanna Amateur Champion

1974 Western Amateur Match & Medal Play Champion

1980 Texas State Open Champion

1981, 1983, 1987 & 1995 United States Ryder Cup Team

1983 U.S. Team vs. Japan

1985 PGA Senior Team Event Champion; Jeremy Ranch Shoot-Out
   (w/Miller Barber)

1987, 1988 World Cup; 1988 Team Champion (w/Mark McCumber)

1988 Captain and Team Member of U.S. Kirin Cup Team

1995 Captain and Team Member of U.S. Dunhill Cup Team

1995 Mastercard Grand Slam of Golf Champion

1999 Captain, United States Ryder Cup Team

1971, 1972, 1973 Collegiate All-American

1971, 1972, 1973 Fred Haskins Award (Outstanding Collegiate Golfer)

1980 Texas Golf Hall of Fame

1984 University of Texas Hall of Honor

1985 Golden Tee Award (Metropolitan Golf Writers)

1989 William Richardson Award (Golf Writers of America)

1991 Ambassador of Golf Award (California Golf Writers)

1991 Bob Jones Award (United States Golf Association)

1995 Texas Sports Hall of Fame

1997 Old Tom Morris Award (Golf Course Superintendents Association)

1997 Distinguished Alumni Award (University of Texas)

1999 Francis Ouimet Award (Massachusetts Government Association)

2000 Harvey Penick Award

2001 Payne Stewart Award (PGA Tour)

In the words of legendary golf writer Grantland Rice:

For when the one great scorer comes to write against your name,
He writes not that you won or lost, but how you played the game.

So it is for Ben's fans, from Austin to Augusta, to Brookline and back, he is a gentleman always and forever a champion.

> *Rob Gillette*
> *Friend, fan, and founder,*
> *Ben Crenshaw's Fan Clubs*
> *(Ben's Battalion and Team Crenshaw)*

To become a member, send correspondence and/or your e-mail address to:

TEAM CRENSHAW
1800 Nueces St.
Austin, Texas 78701

www.bencrenshaw.com

ABOUT THE AUTHORS

Ben Crenshaw began playing golf at the age of six, and after twenty-nine years on the PGA Tour is one of the most beloved figures in sports. Born, raised, and devoted to Austin, Texas, Ben makes his home there with his wife, Julie, and daughters Katherine, Anna Riley, and Claire.

Melanie Hauser spent twenty years covering sports at the *Austin American-Statesman* and the *Houston Post*. An award-winning feature writer and columnist, she has contributed to the *New York Times*, *Golf World*, *Golf Digest*, *Golf Magazine*, and golfweb.com. Now a freelance writer, she lives in Houston, Texas.